Changing Landscapes:
The Ancient Fenland

John Coles & David Hall

1998

Cambridgeshire County Council

WARP (Wetland Archaeology Research Project)

Published by:

Cambridgeshire County Council

&

Wetland Archaeology Research Project

© 1998 John Coles & David Hall

WARP Occasional Paper 13
ISBN 0 9519117 6 7

Cambridgeshire County Council. Education, Libraries & Heritage
ISBN 0 902436 53 8

Cover Illustrations:

Front: *Winter flooding in the Whittlesey Washes*   (photo: David Hall)

Back: *Excavation at Market Deeping*   (photo: John Coles)

Design by David Musgrove
Printed by Short Run Press Ltd., Exeter

Contents

Preface

This book has been written in response to requests, from Fenlanders and others, for a short account of the long history of the Fenland. Archaeologists, historians and geographers have studied aspects of this vast region for many years, but their work has coincided with the gradual loss of the ancient record through drainage and other activities. In the last twenty years, archaeologists have made many discoveries through surveys and excavations in Cambridgeshire, Lincolnshire, Norfolk and Suffolk. These allow us to see more clearly how people lived and worked in the Fenland over the past 6000 years. Their story is presented here, along with an account of how the present landscape has been created by generations of settlers who saw opportunities in the Fenland for hunting, gathering, farming and industry.

Much of the recent work has been supported by English Heritage, and our text also relies on studies carried out by other organisations; a short list appears at the end of the book. Here will also be found some references to more detailed reading, and to places where sites and objects can be seen in and around the Fenland.

July 1998

John Coles
David Hall

Conversion table

We have used metric measurements throughout except where Imperial seemed more appropriate.

one metre	=	about 39 inches
ten metres	=	about 33 feet
100 metres	=	about 109 yards
one kilometre	=	about 0.6 mile
one hectare	=	about 2.5 acres

Chapter 1

More water than land

Fenland – an unendingly flat landscape of dark fields, sluggish rivers, dykes and banks, with infrequent and scattered settlements. This is a popular view of the vast tract of land stretching from Cambridge in the south to Lincoln in the north, and from Peterborough in the west to King's Lynn and Boston in the east. It is the largest area of uninterrupted wetland in England (fig. 1.1), approaching one million acres (400,000 hectares), and has been occupied for thousands of years; our purpose here is to provide an outline and a guide to some of the wondrously rich and surprisingly varied landscapes and ancient sites that have been recognised through decades of research. In setting out the record we hope to show that the 'unendingly flat landscape' was nothing of the sort in the past, and indeed is an unfair description of the Fenland today although the infinite variations are often to be measured in inches rather than yards. When Harry Godwin, a Cambridge botanist, began work in the Fenland, he remarked, incautiously, to a Fenman that he found the area singularly flat; to this the Fenman scornfully replied, 'any fool can appreciate mountain scenery, it takes a man of discernment to appreciate the Fens'.

The Fenland began its chequered existence as a well-watered plain, bounded by chalk to the north, east and south, and by clays and limestone to the west. Prehistoric rivers flowed into the basin and out to the sea. But the land itself was not stable, and has slowly sunk over the millennia. Over the past six thousand years or more, the level of the North Sea has also fluctuated. All of these events created conditions that sometimes brought marine waters flooding into the lowlands, leaving blankets of silt, and sometimes allowed freshwaters to pond and to create extensive beds of peat that covered the land. The silts and peats that we see today in the Fenland are only remnants of once much greater deposits that interfingered with each other, here a layer of peat overlain by silt, and there the reverse; the layers can be very numerous as conditions changed rapidly over the centuries from about 6000 years ago. The final stages of this process created a 'peat fen' in the south, and a 'silt fen' in much of the north and east, as our maps in this book will make clear.

Here and there in the Fenland are islands of old geological formations, where the fen floor was sufficiently elevated to ward off flooding. The islands are numerous in the south, the largest being the Isle of Ely which rises to over 30 metres above sea level. There are many peninsulas and promontories as well, and large numbers of low ridges and banks of sand left by the most ancient rivers and streams. All of

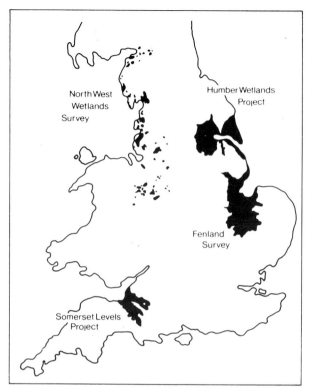

Fig. 1.1 Major wetland areas of England.

these could provide safer and drier surfaces for human occupation. Today, much of the peat fen is near or just below sea level, and the silt fen is about 3 metres above sea level, but these are recent developments. Drainage since the 17th century has caused the peat fen to subside, losing about 5-6 metres of its original height in some areas. As the peat dried, it has shrunk and winds have carried away vast quantities; a 'fen blow' is wondrous to behold. The silt fen, too, has been subject to distortion over past centuries. The effect of it all has been to expose the tops, and then the sides, of old islands and the original fen-edge, where the solid land met the basin peats and silts. The rivers that flow through the peat fen now are heavily banked and many carry water at levels well above the surrounding land. Today, much of the Fenland is intensively used for agriculture and there are many large holdings of the fertile organic soils, the operations dependent upon the continued tight control of water levels.

The landscape of the Fenland has probably changed more in its character than any other landform in Britain. What is now a broadly uniform agricultural landscape was once richly varied, with expanses of open water (meres), wide and shallow rivers prone to flooding, deep and unstable peat bogs of varying heights, wide expanses of silts stretching far upstream and inland from the North Sea shores, and, several thousand years ago, many ridges and islands of clay, gravel and sand still not submerged by the ever-encroaching peats and silts. Within this dynamic and changing landscape, people settled, adapted and exploited the riches that nature guaranteed. Now, archaeologists have combined with geographers, botanists and other scientists to extract and explain the traces left behind by the many generations of nameless people who lived and died in the Fenland over the past six thousand years.

An evocative source of evidence about Fenland lives is the written record of the religious houses established in the southern Fenland from about 650 AD. Guthlac was one of those who sought a solitary life amidst the 'hideous fen of a huge bigness', while others founded religious houses on the islands and edges, at Ely (673), Medeshamstede (Peterborough 655) and Crowland (716). The Venerable Bede identified the place we call Ely in the 8th century as 'the eel district'. By 1086, the settlement at Wisbech could record an annual catch of 33,000 eels, and the fens throughout were yielding innumerable fish, fowl, reed and rush. Sturgeon and swan were reserved for the King, but all people could take ducks, geese, heron and teal by net or trap. Egg collection was another task, and the records tell us of an unnamed boy, probably on stilts, who drowned in the 14th century when searching for ducks' eggs off a fen island. Plants for building and fuel were also abundant, with reeds, rushes and sedges for thatch, and moor-grass for cattle litter, willow withies for baskets, alder for poles and rods, and there were many wild seeds, nuts and berries for seasonal use. Peat itself could be cut and dried for building blocks or for fuel. Summer grazing lands for cattle were valued, being richly enhanced by winter flooding, and in common ownership for all to use. Much of the fen peatland itself was unsuitable for settlement, and islands and the fen-edge were preferred. Farther north, the siltland provided a firmer base for settlement, and the light dry soils could be tilled for crops. Nearer the North Sea, saltmarshes were rich sources for grazing, and salt could be extracted by washing saturated sand to produce brine, then evaporating the liquid. The inland areas of the silt fen were more amenable for grazing and arable cultivation where the silts were thin and peats lay near the surface. By common consent, many such lands were available to all; the 'seven towns of Marshland' in Norfolk formed one such agreeable consortium. A sharing of resources could also help to alleviate the consequences of major floods that continued to plague both peasant farmers and hunter-gatherers over all of the Fenland. Siltland settlers were vulnerable to 'the outrageousness of the sea', engulfing cattle and humans alike by rapid and violent tides. Inland, river outflows could not cope with heavy rainfall or tidal pressure, and peatland activities could be drowned as dykes overflowed or banks broke, and stagnating water lay on the land for weeks.

Yet in all of this, as the decades passed, the records speak of a Fenland well settled, islands and edges providing some measure of permanence, and of traditions of life involving an acceptance of both risk and reward. Until the 17th century, the peat fens of the south were exploited for grazing, and for fishing and fowling; turbaries were established, plants collected and the inhabitants described as 'rude, uncivil and envious to all others'. In the north, the siltlands were equally bountiful, with rich grazing for cattle and sheep, and abundant wildfowl, grasses and fish; the inhabitants were doubtless of comparable temperament to those of the peat fen.

The history of the Fenland through these early days is inextricable from its lifeblood – water. Water provided all the resources, in one way or another, and its taming and control were inevitable. In the Middle Ages, the Wash was a far wider and deeper funnel, some 13 km farther inland than today, and Wisbech was its major port, receiving the waters of the rivers Lark, Cam, Little Ouse, Nene and Western Ouse (fig. 1.2). The Welland and Witham rivers flowed through the siltlands, and all waterways served for transport and communication, carrying cloth, lead and tallow to Ely for example, and stone for religious building at Crowland, Ely, Lincoln and many other places; from Bruges, Cologne and Rouen came merchants with cloth, hides, silk and iron to the fairs at St. Ives and Cambridge. Natural waterways were changed during the 16th century by digging new channels, and in 1631 the great work of 'the exsiccation of the draines' had begun. The Bedford or Hundred Foot River was one of the first of the enormous undertakings to control the water and to drain the land. In both peatlands and siltlands the work went on, with occasional setbacks when the restless floodwaters intruded and drowned cattle, crops and houses. Over time, however, the efforts of the Dutchman Vermuyden and his successors could hardly fail, and the taming of the peatland followed that of the siltland (see Chapter 8). As drainage persisted, shrinkage of the peat fen continued, and pumping out of the water into the new channels became more and more difficult, with rivers embanked to prevent overflow onto the land which in time was lowered below the waterways. Wind, steam, diesel and now electric engines, lifted water from field drains into the elevated rivers. The Fenland today is not a shadow of what it once was, it is a new land. The passing of the old is lamented by some but not by all, as it is only by such operations, carried out over four centuries, that allow us today to live and prosper in the overwhelmingly flat landscape, protected against all but the most severe and unanticipated surges of the sea. But gone are the traditions and lives of the old Fenland, the ways of life once skilfully adapted to a watery existence and deeply entrenched in the patterns established over six thousand years or more.

Studies of the old Fenland have been mostly confined to its exploitation in the Middle Ages and after, but in 1878 a book called The Fenland Past and Present set out a wide view of the natural habitats and of Fenland traditions, already being diminished by the changes brought about by drainage and cultivation. In 1923 a book on The Archaeology of the Cambridge Region placed some emphasis on southern Fenland environments as they had affected human settlement; these and other references are listed at the back of this book. Then in 1932 a group of scientists formed the Fenland Research Committee, for the first time bringing together both archaeologists and natural scientists to focus on Fenland sites and landscapes.

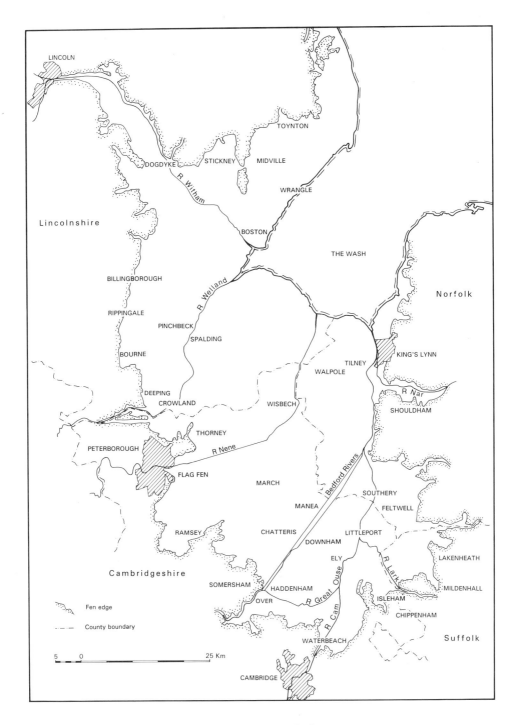

Fig. 1.2 The Fenland with principal rivers and places.

Among the group were Grahame Clark and Harry Godwin, the one an archaeologist, the other a botanist. Godwin set out to study the changing conditions of the southern Fenland, by identifying the phases of peat formation interspersed by marine silt flooding; he said that the Committee had 'the advantage of beginning in total ignorance', not strictly true but nonetheless reflecting the lack of previous scientific work and the almost total lack of knowledge about the earliest people of the Fenland.

Clark and Godwin began their combined work near Shippea Hill in the south-eastern corner of the Fenland. A sandhill was emerging from the shrinking peat and some flint tools had been recovered from a settlement of about 2000 BC on the low ridge overlooking an ancient fen and subsequently buried by later peats. A trench was dug by the team in 1934, nearly 20 feet (6 metres) deep, to observe the various layers of peat and silt, to get plant remains and pollen for environmental reconstruction, and to try to define the precise levels at which human artifacts lay. By great good fortune, three horizons of activity were located; on a deeply-buried sandy riverbank came some flints left by hunter-gatherers about 6500 BC, at a higher level and in peat came some potsherds of settlers who may have been farmers as well as gatherers, about 4200 BC, and high in the section came the occupation of about 2000 BC. By this work, the Committee established the models for Fenland archaeology – deep stratigraphy, excellent conditions for environmental work, and the prospect of finding undisturbed ancient occupation surfaces. Charles Phillips was another of the Fenland pioneers, with particular expertise in mapping, and Gordon Fowler, a locally-based man, was instrumental in reporting on new discoveries. Further work in the later 1930s and on into the post-War years helped identify other horizons, of bog oaks, for example, which indicate a forest floor existing in the centuries around 3000 BC, later drowned and submerged by peat; many have been pulled from the land over the past 30 years or so, as cultivation extends more deeply into the ancient peaty soils (fig. 1.3).

Fig. 1.3 Bog oaks, over 3000 years old, at Holme Fen.

Another formidable result of the Committee's work was its recognition of the abundance of debris from settlements and other activities of the centuries from about 2500 BC to about 500 BC. Many fen-edge ridges already exposed had flints and potsherds scattered over the cultivated fields, and from the peats were recovered a large number of bronze tools and weapons, some in large hoards, as well as human remains. There were records too of wooden trackways, of oak and of pine, originally made to cross the flooded fens but now, by 1930-1960, hindrances to the plough and trencher. One of the achievements of the Committee's work was the recognition, by fieldwork as well as by aerial photography, of extinct river courses surviving now as banks of light-coloured silt meandering across the Fenland, called roddons (fig. 1.4). They represent old river channels, silt-filled, and not wasting away as rapidly as the surrounding peat. Later settlements were often established on roddons, which provided firmer ground, and crops grow differently on the silts. Today, roddons are plainly visible in the lowered fields, and car drivers will feel the effect if speeding across a barely marked roddon. By the time the Fenland Research Committee ceased its operations, an understanding of the peats had been created, but the record was very uneven, and mostly dependent upon events that were wholly directed at other purposes, namely drainage and agriculture. By the mid-1970s, recognition was widespread that the record was inadequate and potentially of national importance.

Fig. 1.4 Aerial photograph of ancient watercourses (roddons) at Warboys Fen. North at Left.

In 1976, one of us (D.H.) was appointed as Fenland Field Officer, to carry out a rapid archaeological survey of the fens of Cambridgeshire. The method adopted was simple – to search the cultivated fields for new exposures of once-buried settlements. At once, the discoveries came: a hunter-gatherer site at Littleport covering over one hectare, an early farming site at Swaffham Prior which yielded 35 stone axes and thousands of flints, a cemetery of burial mounds just emerging from the peat at Borough Fen, and 10 hectares of settlement debris at Chatteris of the closing centuries BC. All of this was capped, in a way, by the discovery of a huge Roman building at Stonea, surviving as a thick spread of rubble, roof tiles and occupation debris. Many more finds were made in the first year or so of this fieldwork, and it was clear that a major effort had to be mounted to carry out comparable work in all of the Fenland. From 1981 to 1988, Fenland Officers worked in Lincolnshire, Norfolk and Cambridgeshire, while other work was done in Suffolk; the Fenland Survey also had an environmental specialist and facilities for radiocarbon dating and other scientific studies. The work was funded by the Department of the Environment, and latterly by English Heritage. From 1989 to 1996 the work was directed more towards the evaluation and protection of certain areas and sites identified during the first phase.

The Fenland as it now survives consists of large areas of 'black fen,' with peaty soils mostly found in the southern part, and expanses of silt fen to the north and east. Almost all of the 400,000 hectare region is under some form of arable agriculture and almost devoid of pasture. By the end of the field-walking phase, in 1988, about 60 percent of the whole area had been walked, and over 2000 ancient sites had been newly identified and recorded. They ranged in date from about 6000 BC up to the 16th century, with over 900 prehistoric, and 800 Romano-British, sites in the total. But there had already been a long period of discovery of ancient sites in the Fenland, and we now outline some of the earlier work and go on to describe the methods of the Fenland Survey of the 1980s.

The earliest maps of the undrained Fenland were made in the 16th and 17th centuries; Dugdale published a plan of the landscape in 1682, after drainage had begun the transformation, dissecting the land with straight channels. Surface peats had already begun to vanish and long-buried ancient land surfaces and mineral deposits of sites, clays and alluvium were beginning to be revealed. But much was still in its original undisturbed condition, sealed and often waterlogged. In the 1870s, the first geological maps of the Fenland were made by Skertchly who also described antiquities discovered by farmers and peat-cutters. Many artifacts must have been lost over the years, unrecognised or unwanted; others were sold to dealers in the 19th century and presumably reside, unlabelled, in various collections. When the Fenland Survey began its work, the officers were able to recognise and record a number of objects gathering dust on farmhouse shelves, or carefully looked-after by interested landowners. These included stone and bronze axes, sherds of pottery, flint tools and a wide variety of more recent bric-a-brac.

The basis of modern work had been established by two significant advances made in the 1930s, as already mentioned. First was the recognition that the sinuous roddons or 'silt hills' of the Fenland are extinct water courses, which, when mapped, reveal earlier drainage patterns. The Soil Survey of England and Wales later extended this work by mapping the roddon system of the prehistoric fens near Ely and elsewhere on a large scale. Secondly came the dating of buried Fenland strata, in 1934, by relating them to archaeological deposits of known age, and later by subjecting them to radiocarbon dating.

Fig. 1.5   The logo of the Fenland Survey.

The Fenland Survey of the 1980s set out to record Fenland archaeology systematically, and to add to the information already known about the topography, soils and roddons. Maps at the 'six-inch' scale (1:10,560) were prepared, marked with existing archaeological information and the roddon-systems as revealed by vertical aerial photographs. In the field, lines 30 metres apart were walked during winter months when land surfaces were weathered (fig. 1.5). Artifacts, mainly of pottery or flint, were collected, and soils and roddons were checked, all new information being recorded on the maps. A selection of soil samples was radiocarbon dated and analysed for environmental evidence.

The database so accumulated was used to reconstruct Fenland landscapes at various periods, using dated soil types and the heights of the fen deposits (fig. 1.6). For

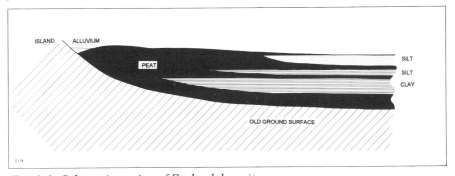

Fig. 1.6   Schematic section of Fenland deposits.

instance, the late Neolithic landscape (about 2500 BC) in the embayment between Ely and Downham Market was mapped from the extent of the grey marine clay then deposited, and the detail of contemporary mudflat drainage channels added by drawing in the roddons. Marine deposits were hemmed in by a landward belt of peat, varying in width in time and place. Another example: in the Iron Age there were no marine deposits south of Ely and the whole embayment was covered with peat, but how thick was it and where was the fen-edge? This can be estimated from a key site at Manea where a small silt roddon lies directly on the old land surface at 2.5 metres above mean sea level (OD). The silt had backed up a channel lying in a now vanished shallow peat so establishing a datum of about 2.5 metres OD for the southern peat fen at that date. From similar information the fen-edge at any date may be estimated and mapped.

The marine mud-flat drainage channels represented by roddon networks are easy enough to recognise. Other drainage channels require careful interpretation; whilst straight ones are undoubtedly man-made, not all crooked watercourses are entirely natural. Location and topography have to be considered. A good example is the Catswater, the pre-1972 county boundary between Cambridgeshire and Northamptonshire. It is referred to on many occasions in the Middle Ages as the northern course of the Nene and it is now represented by a drain meandering along the middle of a gravel peninsula. Natural channels, of course, run either side of peninsulas, not along them. The explanation of the Catswater is that the peninsula was reduced to a narrow strip in the early Middle Ages by the encroaching fens of Peterborough and Thorney lying either side. The rising peat presented drainage difficulties for the main river and this was partly solved by digging the Catswater as a relief along the peninsula, following the edge of Thorney Fen – hence the sinuous nature of the channel along the 4 metre contour. The abbots of Thorney and Peterborough monasteries are likely to have been the initiators of this work.

At March, the artificial but crooked course of the Roman Nene has a different origin. It was created by diverting the river into a channel cut through a narrow neck of mineral soil, so severing the indented island of March. The waters then ran into a natural meandering watercourse on the east, which was deepened and widened, proceeding to Friday Bridge.

Addition of archaeological information brings to life the Fenland landscape maps reconstructed by the methods outlined above. In the following chapters we explain how, for thousands of years, successive generations of fen-dwellers exploited the challenge of the continually changing landscape.

Chapter 2

The first Fenlanders

In the several thousand years since people first settled in the Fenland, their broken and discarded objects have lain mostly undisturbed in the soil. Over time, objects of wood and cloth have decayed away unless waterlogged conditions permitted survival. Bones too, the residues of countless meals, have sometimes perished although many sites provide good conditions for survival. Of plant foods such as cereals and fruits, little is often preserved although analyses of the pollen surviving in peat tell us about the existence and character of such fragile remains. The abandoned camp sites, and small settlements with shelters mostly of wood, have also been subject to decay, so the only surviving elements may be post- or stake-holes, hearths with burnt soils and stones, gullies and pits, and middens with broken pottery, bone and antler, discarded stone tools and general debris. Some sites discovered by the Fenland Survey had most of these elements, which allowed a reasonably detailed reconstruction to be attempted; other sites were badly disturbed by the plough or by exposure to natural weathering, and conditions on some were so severe that only a scatter of flints remained. In such cases, it is difficult to be certain about interpretations.

There were many thousands of occupation sites in the Fenland, dating from the last six thousand years; many have been destroyed over the past two centuries, but many remain. Some very old sites, deeply buried by silts and peats, will probably never be found; younger sites, lying higher up in the sediments, will be exposed by ploughing or other disturbances and will be destroyed. But it is not only age and depth that matter, as the character of the original site and its conditions of abandonment will also determine what remains. The oldest traces of Fenland occupation are a good example of these factors. For these, we have only stray finds of stone tools, found entirely by accident during deep diggings, or by erosion of river gravel; no living floors or settlements have been identified; they would be on the floor of the Fenland basin, near stream courses where animals might come to drink or browse. At this time the Fenland was but one of a series of low-lying areas stretching eastwards across a land that is now the North Sea; Britain was a small peninsula of a great landmass that is now Europe and Asia. The Fenland finds from these very early occupations consist of flint tools, often handaxes (fig. 2.1), some made perhaps 500,000 years ago, dropped or abandoned as hunter-gatherers moved across the low plain in their quest for food or good camping sites. Such Palaeolithic (Old Stone Age) axes as have been found appear to

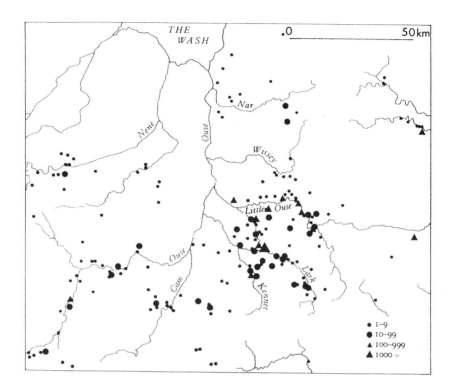

Fig. 2.1 (lower) Handaxe from Feltwell, one of over 200 found in a gravel pit at Shrub Hill. Length 30 cm.

(upper) Distribution of Old Stone Age tools from the southern Fenland.

concentrate around ancient river and stream courses; at Sutton in Cambridgeshire a likely encampment was on the edge of the basin, and at Feltwell in Norfolk the discovery of over 240 axes and some flakes suggests that an occupation site was near, perhaps already disturbed by glacial action before gravel digging destroyed any surviving living or working floor. We may live in hope that some day an intact site will be found, but it is only much later occupations that have been securely identified along the fen-edge. At Methwold in Norfolk, an observant farmer noted some long flint blades during dyke-cutting; they probably came from a campsite on the edge of a freshwater lake. The age of this site is likely to be somewhere in the range 9000-6000 BC, when the Fenland basin was mostly forested, and game of deer, boar and beaver was abundant. Communities of hunters and gatherers were probably small, and permanent settlements sparse.

The precise extent and survival of the ancient Fenland forests is not known, but it seems likely that until about 4000 BC there were few efforts to make many clearances. Hunter-gatherers of the forests and rivers in the period 6000-4000 BC are identifiable by their flint tools and debris, and the survey work as well as many private collections demonstrate how widely spread were the territories of these shadowy people. Most of their sites lie buried by peat and silt which submerged the low knolls and ridges that provided some slight elevation above the Fenland floor. Along the edge of the basin, and at places where streams and rivers flowed into the Fenland itself, many occupation sites have been identified. However, we think that the population was very low and that many of the small scatters of flints might represent the work of only a very few mobile groups, perhaps only 3-4 persons camping for a short time, preparing or renewing their tools, before moving on (fig. 2.2). Larger spreads of flints, over wide areas of sandy ridges, or more densely clustered, might represent long periods of regular visits to favoured locations rather than any major concentrations of people gathered together. Most sites were near watering places, and the bow and arrow was likely to be the main weapon for killing animals. Collection of plant food, berries, roots, seeds and greens, would be a major activity as well. Flint and wood were the main materials for equipment, and flint technology was well-practised, with knives, scrapers, borers and arrow tips, produced from nodules collected from the Fenland gravels and from weathered chalk of the eastern and southern uplands.

The sites of these Mesolithic (Middle Stone Age) hunter-gatherers are now known from the south-east Fenland, at Methwold for example, where three clusters of chipping debris and tools on the western tip of the Catsholm ridge must represent temporary camps. The same kind of evidence was found at Hockwold on Decoy Farm sandhill, and at Lakenheath in Suffolk there were stakeholes and crescentic-shaped outlines in the sand, perhaps the remnants of slender shelters. On the Peacock's Farm ridge at Shippea Hill a few hearths were noted in excavations, and the environment was a dense forest that had at one time been partly cleared by fire, possibly to drive game but more probably to create openings for more abundant

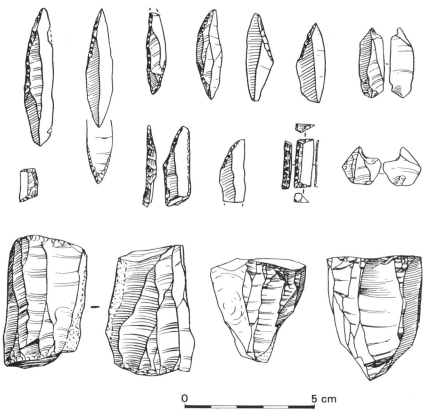

0 ———————————— 5 cm

Fig. 2.2 Some flint tools and cores of the Middle Stone Age from Peacock's Farm.

growth of browse shrubs and grasses, thus attracting game like deer, elk and aurochs. At Soham, the Survey identified a concentration of flint scatters on sandy soil, newly-exposed by wastage; among the abundant Mesolithic material were several core axes (fig. 2.3). In the northern Fenland, traces of similar age are less well-known, because inundations from the Wash have buried entire landscapes. At Cowbit, for example, the contemporary surface is beneath as much as 10 metres of sediments. Between Boston and Horncastle, however, a ridge projects into the basin, and was a focus for early occupation. The landscape was probably forested, with oak, lime and elm, but some peat was forming in low waterlogged parts of the basin (fig. 2.4), and at East and West Keal, sandy hillocks provided good vantage points for temporary occupations by hunter-gatherers. At Midville, such an occupation lies mostly sealed beneath peat, itself covered by marine-based silts. The identification of sites like these where preservation might be good must be a priority for the future.

One of the major questions in Fenland prehistory, as elsewhere, is the relationship that existed between the hunter-gatherers who worked the forests and river banks

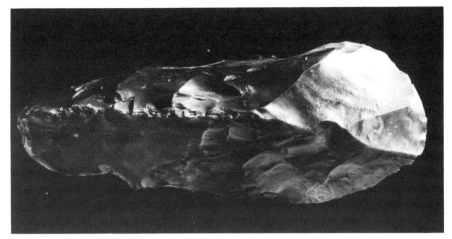

Fig. 2.3 Core axe from the Soham cluster of sites. Length 10 cm.

in the decades around 4000 BC and the 'first farmers', people who began to make inroads into the forests and to establish Neolithic (New Stone Age) farming regimes. It appears that some slight but nonetheless significant agricultural practices began to appear in the Fenland about 4000 BC, and it is as likely that such activities were carried out by the hunter-gatherers, learning some new technologies from their neighbours to the south and east, as by wholly immigrant groups moving into the forested zones of the Fenland. By whatever mechanism, clearances and cultivation of plants, and the pasturing of domesticated animals, began to take place in the Fenland in the centuries from about 4000 BC. Conditions in the Fenland around this time were already fluid, with vast sweeps of clastic sediments (marine-based silts in the main) submerging much of the basin and spreading up the major river systems in both the north (the ancient Witham) and the south (the ancestral Ouse and a forerunner of the Nene drainage). There were few major formations of freshwater peats until about 3400 BC. The hunting and gathering economies were well-based to take advantage of the changing conditions, although over time vast amounts of forested dryland were lost to the swamping peats.

The archaeological surveys of the 1980s augmented the record of these activities and responses in very substantial ways. By 3000 BC, the Fenland was transformed by both fresh and marine waters, and peat was forming in many riverine backwaters and in deeper channels, just as marine and brackish-based silts had encroached on much of the lowlands around the Wash (fig. 2.5). This general picture, however, masks the variety of local environments that became available, from sea-based mudflats, saltmarsh, reed and sedge fen, fen carr, woodland on basin elevations, oak and lime forests along the fen-edge. The wealth of natural resources available to hunter-gatherers and first farmers alike was probably as varied and abundant as anywhere in a country that had by now become detached from the continent.

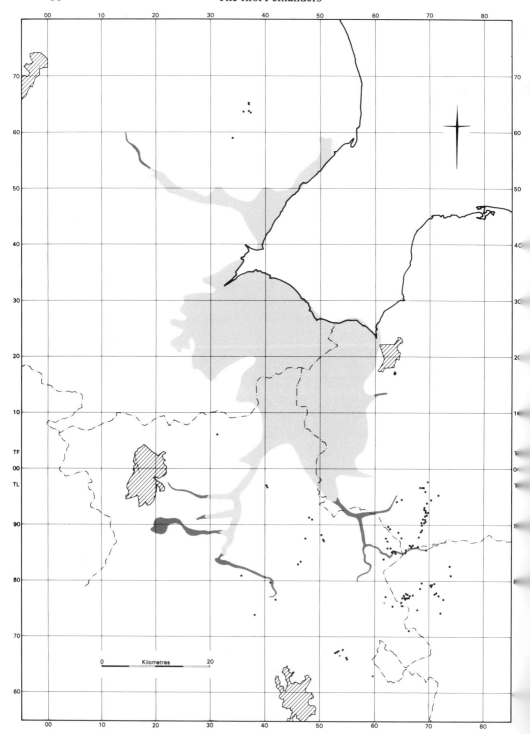

Fig. 2.4 Distribution of Middle Stone Age sites on a map of the fen landscape of
about 5000 BC. Dark tone peat, light tone silt.

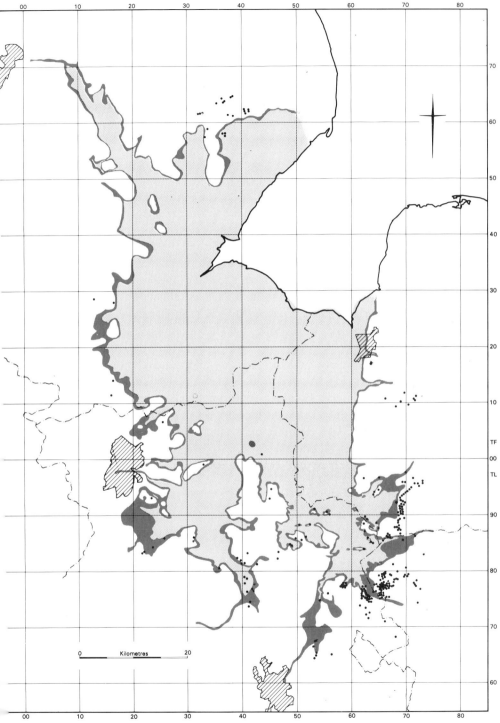

Fig. 2.5 Distribution of New Stone Age sites on a map of the fen landscape of about 2500 BC. Dark tone peat, light tone silt.

Fig. 2.6 Polished stone axe from Fordham, length 27 cm.

The evidence for settlement consists once again of scatters and spreads of flint tools and the debris of knapping, with polished stone axes (fig. 2.6), bowl-shaped pottery and the occasional artifact of bone, antler or wood where survival has been good. But other evidence also exists, in the form of earthworks and ditches of community-based monuments. The general spread of settlement or activity debris in the period from about 4000 BC is much more dense than that of the preceding Mesolithic phase. In the north, a scatter of sites along the fen-edge, especially around Stickney, may only represent some minor interest in the fen on the part of dryland-based communities of the Wolds. The many long burial mounds (barrows) of the Wolds may have been central to settlement although occupation at East Keal, where a characteristic flint assemblage was found, may indicate something more than a transitory interest. At Tattershall Thorpe, upslope of the fen, excavation revealed pits and postholes, pottery and flints in abundance, the latter distinguished by pieces used exclusively for meat, hide, wood, bone, antler or plants; this site probably had the fen-edge and fen basin as part of its territorial round. Along the western fen-edge, settlement of this period is not well-represented by the Survey results but several important sites indicate that much more remains submerged by peat or silt. At Dowsby, for example, excavation of a burial mound of about 2000 BC uncovered an array of postholes which appear to be a part of a rectangular building dated by pottery to the Neolithic, perhaps around 2500 BC.

At Etton, an enclosure with a waterlogged ditch was shown to have been a centre for settlement and for ceremony around 3000 BC (fig. 2.7). Inside the enclosure, which was about 140 by 180 metres in size, were many postholes and pits, and the bones of cattle; cereal pollen was recovered in the analysis of environmental samples. The interpretation was obvious – the settlement of a farming community. But also within the enclosure were many small deposits, pits with stone axes, antler, pottery, hazelnuts and acorns; these may have been offerings to the powers outside normal human activity. The ditch also contained material that appeared to be deliberately placed, including human skulls. Etton may have served a dual purpose, for episodic ceremonial and domestic functions, perhaps as a seasonal focus for the small communities along the western fen-edge. Nearby was another ditched area called Etton Woodgate, with flint work and pottery, and a slightly later pit dug for charcoal production. A cursus monument (a linear banked processional way) lies near these sites and the whole complex, in use over perhaps

Fig. 2.7 Etton. Part of the waterlogged ditch.

1000 years, suggests that the location was a place of power and control for the farming societies of the region.

Not far away, at Fengate, a long series of unconnected excavations has now been pulled together to suggest that in the centuries after about 4000 BC there had existed some form of land organisation, focused on a particular land strip from dryland into wetland. Ditches upslope may represent a droveway for animal control, but leading towards fen-edge land where there was a ditched rectangular enclosure with internal bank and no formal entrance; farther on towards the fen was a small building with a scatter of flint blades, a sickle blade, a fragment of a stone axe and other debris, and down near the fen-edge was a burial pit containing an adult male with an arrowhead in his spine, an adult female and two children (fig. 2.8). All of these structures may be concerned with death – ceremonial enclosure, mortuary house with special offerings, and burial pit.

The full extent of settlement involving some measure of cultivation and pastoralism during the centuries from about 4000 BC onwards is not known at present, and many sites must lie awaiting discovery. There are a few traces on the western edge although local collectors around Ramsey made many finds from locations now lost. At Honey Hill, a small gravel outcrop overlooked a narrow fen in a prime situation for access to both wetland and dryland resources. Ploughing had removed all structural remains, but a stone axe and many thousands of flints, some of them burnt, indicate an occupation, probably seasonal, over many years. The gravel may have been a good source for flint tools, made on the site. Across the narrow

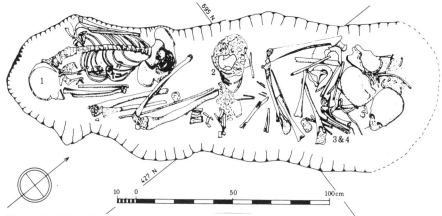

Fig. 2.8 A burial pit from Fengate with four bodies interred.

fen were smaller camps on the opposing gravels. A major concentration of settlement has been identified on the March-Manea-Chatteris drylands, with many scatters of flints, and some stone axes, bone and pottery, but little in the way of structure other than a ditched earthwork partly overlain by Neolithic debris. That this area of the southern fens was something more than merely an offshoot, seasonally visited, by people more firmly attached to the upslope drylands is suggested by the recent discoveries by field-walking and aerial photography of several earthen long barrows and enclosures in the Sutton-Haddenham area (see fig. 3.5). These had been wholly submerged by peat.

One of the mounds, about 50 metres long and 20 metres wide, was examined and shown to have a complex history, with a long mortuary-chamber made of huge oak planks, and a ditched curving facade at the entry to the chamber. At least five bodies had been placed in the chamber, and outside it were several complete pots and reddish stones. The chamber was buried beneath a turf mound and then the long barrow was created over the entire funerary monument. Expectations were high that the good preservation might have revealed decoration in the form of carvings or painted surfaces, but no trace was found. The three long barrows so far discovered lay on a small island in the developing fen, and to the south, at Haddenham Delphs, a larger island had a causewayed enclosure of over eight hectares, one of the largest known in Britain. A palisade lay inside the ring of an interrupted ditch, and at the main entrance there were human skulls and other offerings deposited. Sites such as this probably represent focal points for wide communal contact and activities designed to cement relationships among groups of people otherwise wholly engaged on normal and isolated pursuits.

Centres such as this and another at Great Wilbraham may have attracted people from the rivers Cam and Lark area of the south-eastern fen. In this region, the scatters of flints, axes and pottery are very abundant. In the Swaffhams, for example, many sites lie on gravels and sands along ancient river courses, and burial mounds may well be revealed by further wastage of the peats. At Soham and Isleham, further concentrations of presumed seasonal settlements have been noted, some on small islands and others on narrow peninsulas. Farther north, as the fen-edge turns north through Feltwell and Methwold, more scatters of flints and pottery have been recovered, with particular concentrations at Feltwell on sandhills at the fen-edge. Sealed by peat, sites all along the south-eastern Fenland continue to appear and known distributions will be extended and reinforced. What the sites represent is less clear, and there is probably a variety of purposes represented in the scatters and spreads. On some, the abundance of burnt flint as well as flaking debris suggests that they combined cooking activities and the preparation of new or renewed flint tools. Little in the way of structural evidence survives, but at the site of Hurst Fen near Mildenhall, excavations in the late 1950s showed that occupation covered about 1.5 hectares, and had resulted in the digging of many pits and postholes; of house outlines no trace survived, and the bones of cattle, sheep, horse and pig were badly decayed. The site, of about 3000 BC, had been truncated by ploughing. Nonetheless, the fine flintwork, of leaf arrowheads, large leaf-shaped points, awls, knives and scrapers, and the round-based pottery (fig. 2.9), some decorated, and the heavy stone querns and hammers, all suggest

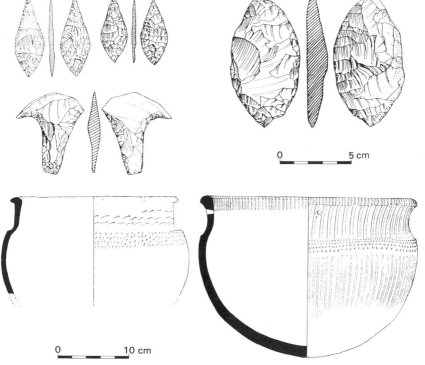

Fig. 2.9 Pottery and flint implements from Hurst Fen, Mildenhall.

that the site had been a major settlement, perhaps permanent. On the other hand, it may have been like the Etton occupation, across the Fenland, combining both domestic and ceremonial activities.

Perhaps major sites such as these are best seen as focal points for those communities who had begun the process of combining the advantages of a wild Fenland life with those of an existence more firmly wedded to particular patches of land for pasture or cultivation. Lives would depend on a mobility more marked than we might ordinarily consider for an agricultural community. At darker times of the year, when the growing season had ended, food collections made and stored, or when stored supplies were running low, communal gatherings for warmth, celebration or commiseration, and general contact between competing or collaborating parties would be essential to avoid friction. For whatever reason, and perhaps there were several, parts of the Fenland had now come under some measure of social organisation, but the land was certainly not under control and the onslaught of Fenland waters was now underway.

Chapter 3

Living on the edge

By about 2600 BC, large areas of the Fenland had been swamped by freshwater peats, particularly strongly developed in the south-west, but from this time onwards for another 500 years or so, marine-based deposition of silts dominated the whole of the Fenland, overriding the peaty expanses and clogging the valleys (fig. 3.1). In the embayments, where rivers flowed, and along the margins of the fen, peat remained exposed and continued to form with the severely impeded drainage. The archaeological surveys over these landscapes were obviously hindered, as ever, by subsequent deposits but along the fen-edge, and on a number of ridges and islands in the fen, the continued presence of people is attested by scatters of flints, stone axes, pottery, and by two new types of archaeological evidence, burnt mounds and burial mounds.

From the Stickney ridge in the north a number of stone and flint tools were recorded along the margin of the fen or on low islands in the fen, probably representing seasonal interests in the wetland. Stone axes and reed-cutting flint blades indicate some of the activities. At East Kirkby, occupation may have been of longer duration and flints and pottery at Stickford may also indicate a permanent interest in the location. To the west, the river Witham was confined to its wide valley although the course of the river within it was constantly changing. At Dogdyke, where the river meets the Kyme Eau, an island now called Chapel Hill was occupied, with flints, burnt flints, and pottery marking the settlement. The place was near the confluence of tidal waters and freshwaters, so permanent occupation is unlikely. Excavations showed further evidence of the settlement itself and the remains of a structure made of two parallel rows of wooden posts, set about 1.5 metres apart and running for at least 20 metres away from the occupied area, probably down and off the island if comparisons with other double-rowed post alignments in southern Britain are valid. The purpose of such alignments is unknown, and on some alignments various artifacts, such as tools or weapons, were laid between or beside the posts. The Dogdyke site may well hold new surprises for us.

Down the western fen-edge much of the relevant landscape remains buried but occupations represented by flints and pottery have been noted where exposures of the ancient fen-edge occur. Inland, at Billingborough, an excavation demonstrated a permanent presence in about 1500 BC; a ditched enclosure protected the settlement and there were raised granaries. On the fen-edge at Dowsby, a cemetery

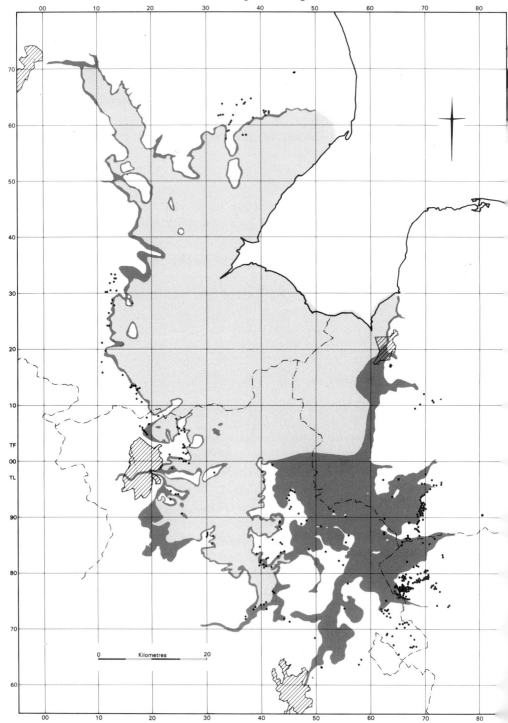

Fig. 3.1 Distribution of Early Bronze Age burial mounds (red) and other sites (black)
on a map of the fen landscape of about 1800 BC. Dark tone peat, light tone silt.

of burial mounds, ploughed flat, was found along with occupation debris of flint and pottery. Excavation and further survey indicated that the settlement of about 2000 BC extended over two hectares, and beneath, as noted in Chapter 2, the postholes of an earlier building were identified. Another settlement was found at Rippingale, and farther south a sandy island at Pinchbeck had been occupied, with pits and hollows marking some form of activity around 2000 BC, and also some centuries later when it is possible that salt-making was carried out here; if so, this is one of the earliest of such sites in the Fenland. Certainly the conditions, with tidal waters near, were suitable. At Thurlby, a settlement on gravel was identified and a major occupation of about 2000 BC was recorded from the margins of Deeping Fen with burial mounds, flint and pottery scatters. A logboat 14 metres long was found in 1839 and might be a part of this activity; it cannot be dated now as it was used as firewood soon after discovery. At the Deepings, several cemeteries of barrows were recorded in the Survey, five at Market Deeping and eight at Deeping St. Nicholas. Other cemeteries lie within six kilometres of these.

One of the St. Nicholas barrows was excavated and revealed a very complex history. On a gravel promontory, an abandoned settlement became the focus for the ritual. A pit was dug for a young child, buried in a shroud in a wooden coffin, with the grave marked by posts and surrounded by eight concentric rings of stakes (fig. 3.2). The site remained like this for perhaps 25 years, and the uprights rotted. Then a mound was erected over the site, with a quarry ditch around. A ring of posts was put up around the mound and two shrouded adults were later put into the side of the mound. One adult had a jet beaded drawstring on his shroud. Then the mound was enlarged, with another ring ditch, and several cremations were put

Fig. 3.2 Excavation of a burial mound at Deeping St Nicholas.

into the side and others just outside the mound, some with pottery perhaps containing food or drink, some as tokens only. Another site, at St. James, was partly excavated in order to work out how the major part could be preserved from damage. It proved to contain various gullies from roundhouses, with pits and postholes from other elements of the settlement (fig. 3.3).

Fig. 3.3 Bronze Age round house gullies from Deeping St James.

The Crowland peninsula just south of the Deepings once had equally significant settlements and cemeteries of the centuries around 2000 BC, but much was destroyed in the 19th century, with records of 'rude pottery ... flint spearheads and arrowheads ... a bronze celt', and a tantalising note of 'a great mound raised upon the earth', perhaps a long barrow like Haddenham.

Borough Fen and Thorney represent further examples of a multitude of Bronze Age burial mounds of the centuries around 2000 BC; many of these were identified by the Survey, in some cases as the tops of the mounds began to emerge from the wasting peats. The cemeteries were placed on gravel and sand promontories and edges of the fens, which were extremely wet with many minor streams and other channels snaking their way through the sodden peats. The barrows were about 15-20 metres in diameter, and 1-2 metres high, many of them being ditched; aerial photographs suggest that a ditched field system at Borough Fen may be contemporary, and that the ancient Welland river was nearby. Other similar cemeteries have been recorded (fig. 3.4), as well as cropmarked enclosures and

Fig. 3.4 Burial mounds at Haddenham, emerging from peat.

droveways at Thorney. These groups of barrows may indicate how the territory of the south-western Fenland was divided up, each settlement with its dryland, fen-edge, fen and stretch of river or stream as a resource base to be managed and doubtless guarded against outsiders. There is little evidence at this time for the need for any major protective earthworks or palisades for settlements, and it is likely that communities were small and not seriously engaged in major communal works. However, this view may be too simple, when we consider the results and interpretations of work at Fengate near Peterborough.

Excavations at a very large scale have been underway here for over 20 years, and the results have provided much new information about agricultural activities of the centuries around and well after 2000 BC. At one of the sites, called Newark Road, a series of ditches, often paired, has been shown to represent a complex system of stock control, with droveways leading down into the fen, and small square or rectangular fields used for holding and grazing. These all were in use for a long time, with many recuttings and adjustments. The complexity of the Newark Road system suggests that this was more than a simple localised mechanism for movement of animals, but functioned more as stockyards for a larger population. Here, at times when grazing patterns were to be changed, from dryland to wetland pastures, cattle and sheep and their owners were brought together and, in the small paddocks served by a major droveway with multiple entrances, animals could be penned awaiting exchange or barter, auctioned in effect. Thus large numbers of stock could be handled in sequence, controlled on arrival, maintained during the

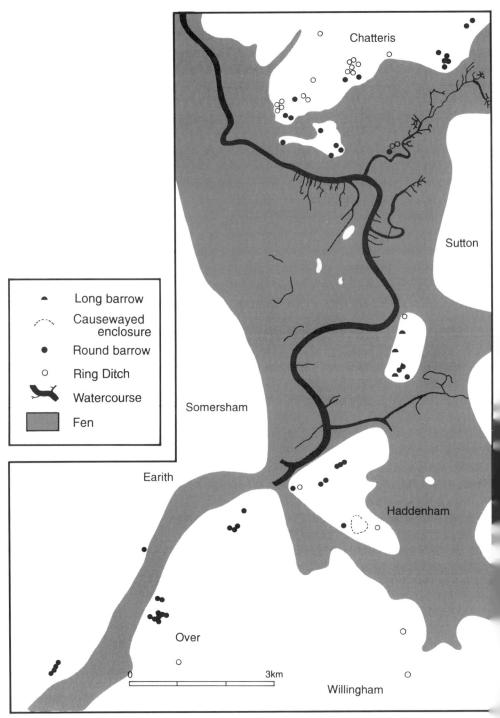

Fig. 3.5 Map of burial mounds and other monuments located along the prehistoric River Ouse. Dark tone peat.

period of assembly, parcelled out and then marshalled ready for the drives to new pastures and new owners. This system, developed over time from much simpler and more locally-based droveways, may well have not fully emerged until the centuries near 1000 BC, but its origins lie in an early conception of the dryland-wetland system for seasonal grazing, for control over particular land strips gaining access to both land forms, and for the perceived need to ensure good relationships with all who depended upon or who wished to benefit from communal efforts. At Fengate, we can see the forerunner of medieval stock-handling systems, revealed and interpreted by major excavations of a landscape now almost wholly obliterated by the growth of modern Peterborough. More recent excavations at the Fengate Depot site exposed part of a ditched system of a comparable nature but with coaxial ditches.

South of this apparent centre of activity, the more localised community work is again evident in the landscapes of the centuries around 2000 BC. At Ramsey the Survey identified another cemetery of burial mounds, placed on a narrow peninsula overlooking the wide fen and with traces of settlement debris on adjacent promontories. The whole of the southern fen-edge, from Chatteris across to Mildenhall, has a scatter of comparable sites. The Chatteris island itself has many barrows, flint scatters, cropmarks of field systems and also some stray finds of bronze tools such as axes; a rapier was recovered from a logboat over a century ago. Many of the barrow cemeteries are small, three to six mounds on the fen-edge, with their settlement scatters behind on the drier lands. Droveways and large enclosures may well be associated with some of these seemingly isolated and small centres of activity.

The complex at Over and Haddenham is remarkable, with large barrows (20-30 metres diameter) in well-defined cemeteries (fig. 3.5); sporadic examination of several has yielded cremations and inhumations, pottery and arrowheads. On one of the island cemeteries, a rectangular ditched enclosure may have served as an assembly point for the ceremonies. It is likely that transport of the dead was an important element in the dedications, and logboats, such as one from Warboys (see fig. 3.8), may have served to provide the physical as well as emotional links between mainland and islands in the fens. But the fen itself served purposes other than wetland resources and summer grazing. The deep dark peats, and streams, received offerings from at least 2000 BC onwards and probably much earlier. These could be stone tools, metal objects, pottery, animals and indeed humans. From Grunty Fen at Wilburton, three bronze axes and a gold torc were recovered during peat digging in 1844 (fig. 3.6). Along the eastern fen-edge and out in the fen itself have come a series of human bodies. One of the first to be investigated was near Methwold where a young female had come to rest, face down, wearing a bracelet of jet beads. About a dozen comparable bodies are now known to have been put into the fen in the centuries around 2500 BC. Several were put out near the Hilgay-Southery island in Norfolk, in sedge carr or reedswamp conditions. Other offerings

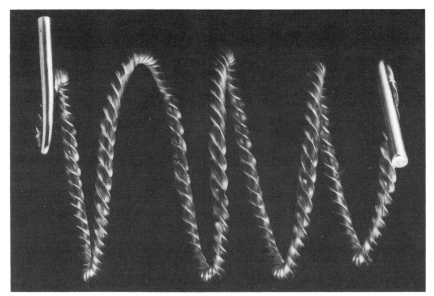

Fig. 3.6 Solid gold coiled torc or armlet from Grunty Fen.

were confined to fen-edge locations; at Burnt Fen near Littleport a pit had been dug and filled with potsherds and antler stubs, in an act well beyond our comprehension. The settlements of this period are scattered along the fen-edge which in the south-eastern Fenland was a convolution of peninsulas, small embayments and multiple islands.

At Soham, the Survey and subsequent excavation identified a very large area of occupation badly disturbed by ploughing but still represented by fragmentary hearths, many thousands of flints including arrowheads, scrapers and awls, and some potsherds. This probably reflects the fact that the area had been the focus of consistent activity over a very long time, no one particular episode necessarily being dominant; the location was the reason rather than any special event or major place of assembly. The Snail river valley was another area for settlement at this time, with barrow cemeteries at Chippenham, occupation on promontories overlooking the stream, and other cemeteries at Snailwell nearby. Many of the barrows were excavated long ago. Settlement scatters at Isleham lie at different levels on the peninsula, the earlier lower down, the later forced upwards by the rising fen in the centuries from about 2000 BC.

More detail is forthcoming from work done at West Row and Mildenhall, where the fen-edge is fragmented into numerous small islands and promontories. A site of about 2200 BC at Fifty Farm contained the bones of sheep, cattle, pig and deer as well as many flint tools, and a slightly later settlement just inland from the river Lark contained evidence for barley and emmer wheat as well as domestic animal bone. Beside the river a spread of burnt flint was associated with a wooden trough

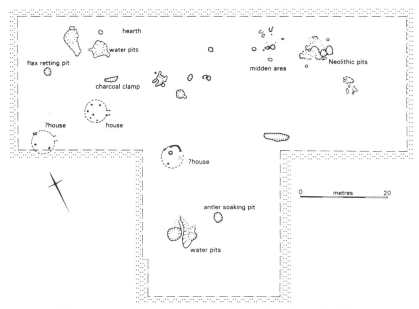

Fig. 3.7 Plan of the Bronze Age settlement at West Row, Suffolk.

lined with withies and dated to 2200 BC. A settlement at West Row, dated around 1600 BC (fig. 3.7), has provided much-needed detail for the activities of fen-edge groups consisting of round houses, water pits serving as wells, pits for flax retting and antler soaking, a charcoal clamp, and much domestic debris of potsherds, flint tools in great variety, heavy stone tools, bone and antler tools. Cattle were the preferred animals for food, with sheep, pig and dog bones also present along with deer and fish. Emmer and spelt wheat, barley and flax were grown. The local environment was scrub and wet woodland, with wet grassland. This period of prehistory is called the Bronze Age, but it will be clear that, for the Fenland, the possession and eventual burial or loss of bronze objects (fig. 3.8) was but a small part of the whole series of activities carried out by the communities from about 2000 BC to about 700 BC.

Away from the tangled fen of the south-east, the edge between dryland and wetland was more recognisable to the north, where off-edge islands were not so numerous. From Hockwold to Northwold there is a string of sites which must indicate an interest in the resources of both upslope and fen conditions, although we are not certain if the sites represent much more than temporary and seasonal occupations. But wherever the mineral soil now protrudes through the wasting peats, flint debris can be seen and it is tempting to suggest that it was the developing fen itself that provided the attraction for occupation. Fish, fowl, wild plant food and summer grazing were the resources sought. The scatters and spreads of stone tools lie only 100 - 200 metres apart at Feltwell, and often are closer; the material consists of flint tools and flaking debris, pottery, burnt flint and occasional bone.

Fig. 3.8   *(right) Logboat from Warboys found in 1910. This contemporary*
          llustration can be viewed from the top or bottom.

          (left) Rapier from West Row with parts of scabbard made of wood.
          Length about 40cm.

Burnt flint occurs in such profusion on many sites that some particular activity must be involved; a site at Feltwell Anchor was excavated where the burnt material survived as a low mound of burnt flint and charcoal, out in the fen away from the fen-edge. Beneath the mound were several pits and an inhumation of a young female was in a grave cut through the mound; she had lain in a coffin of wood. Nearby was a deep pit containing an alder trough, and it is likely that some form of steaming had been carried out here, perhaps steam baths for purification, perhaps for the processing of hides. Another burnt mound was examined at Northwold on the fen-edge. Here the mound was tightly crescentic surrounding a rectangular pit lined with alder boards. Other pits showed signs of periodic cleaning-out, and domestic animal bones and potsherds of about 2000 BC were recovered from the mound material. Some of the burnt flint on many sites may represent the detritus of cooking pits; where pits could be dug into soils that held water, a natural boiling pit was created, perhaps lined by wooden slats or stones or woven branches. Stones, heated in an adjacent fire and dropped into the water, would soon bring it to the boil, as shown by many experiments. Upon abandonment, the remains of a hearth, a shallow pit, and numerous shattered and burnt stones, are all that survive until the plough obliterates hearth and pit, leaving only spreads of fire-crazed flint and fragments of other stones.

Fig. 3.9 Reconstruction of a burial ceremony of the Bronze Age.

All of this varied amount of evidence from the centuries around 2000 BC, representing only a small sample of the multiplicity of sites that once existed during the thousand years of activity, speaks of the dynamism of the Fenland. Our information suggests that by now the last of the great woodlands was cleared, that cereal cultivation was a serious activity, but that the pasturing and management of livestock was a dominant element in the lives of almost everyone. The harvests from the wilder lands of the fen and remnant woodlands were still important. And the fen, extending its grasp over the land with each passing decade, could hardly fail to impress those dependent upon its renewing powers and its strength of waters. This may have persuaded people to make special recognition of the wetland, in the positioning of the monuments for their dead (fig. 3.9), and in offering to the darkness of the waters some of the most precious objects of the communities, including humans themselves.

Chapter 4

Responding to change

With the passage of time, the character of the Fenland changed. Around 2000 BC the influence of the sea had been dominant over much of the basin. By 1000 BC, freshwater peats had overwhelmed vast expanses of the Fenland, burying the spreads of silt and over-riding low islands, peninsulas and the ancient fen-edge, sealing both settlements and burial monuments. The changes were profound and to the inhabitants of the Fenland the pace was without doubt noticeable within a lifetime, as the swamping conditions over-rode traditional pastures, clogged ancient routes, and altered the character of the resources from the wild. The waterlogging of the basin was complete by about 1100 BC; Chatteris, Stonea and Manea were now islands for the first time, and the old fen-edge in the east, at Feltwell and Methwold, was submerged by peat. In the north-west, from Bourne into the Witham valley and across to Toynton, peat formed over the old fen-edge and buried parts of the vast silt fen. In such conditions it is likely that economic systems had to be based on livestock as a dominant element in the regime; settlements excavated yield cattle bones as well as those of sheep, pig and dog. Areas well upslope and drained were used for cultivation, and the yields from the watercourses and fens would have been an important part of the food supplies, as well as providing materials for buildings, fences and equipment.

The settlements identified by archaeological survey and other discoveries made over the years that relate to this time are not as abundant as those of the preceding centuries. This may be a reflection of a diminution of interest in a Fenland existence due to the more extreme swamping conditions, or to our inability to recognise and date sites of this period. Scatters of flints, including burnt flints, are generally assigned to a period well before the centuries around 1000 BC, just as the multitude of round burial mounds and ring ditches are thought to represent traditions of an earlier age. Be that as it may, there is nonetheless ample evidence that interest in the Fenland was still intense, but taking its form in ways that were new.

In the upper Witham Valley, the debris from a settlement at Washingborough, with pottery, antler, bone and wooden objects, may relate to the discoveries of various logboats and metal tools and weapons recovered from the valley peats, but there is little structural evidence to allow greater precision. At Hagnaby Lock, Stickford, on the northern fen-edge, a sand island was occupied in the centuries around 1000 BC; a tidal creek flowed nearby, and there may have been salt-making operations here. Various ditches and ard-marks and pits suggest a slightly earlier phase of activity, with open grassland near at hand. Later, a small pit was dug and sherds of 12 different pots were placed concentrically within it, in some symbolic act. Salt-water was now close to the now-ancient Billingborough site, and a squarish enclosure was constructed, probably associated with the salt-making industry. Farther south, at Dowsby, salt-making was underway by a tidal stream, and the occupation deposits examined so far have yielded domestic debris including the bones of cattle, sheep, pig, horse and dog. At Pointon, too, scatters of contemporary pottery are known, so this western edge may not have been as inhospitable as sometimes imagined. From Morton southwards to Bourne, there are traces of activity and a larger settlement was established near the headwaters of the creeks of the Glen and Bourne Eau; a ridge at Thurlby was chosen for another settlement just tucked away from the fen-edge on a gravel knoll. Another rectangular enclosure at Borough Fen, near the earlier barrow cemetery, may be part of a settlement of about 1000 BC with ditched droveways and paddocks for animals; few details are so far available. An oak-built trackway in the area probably relates to fen exploitation.

At West Deeping, aerial photographs and complementary fieldwork have exposed a remarkable complex, of a coaxial ditched system along the fen-edge of the Welland Valley. Droveways and stockyards probably mark a series of individual farmsteads, each with an enclosure, small yards and inter-connected droveways. It is estimated that 3,000-6,000 sheep may have been managed within such a system covering 250 hectares.

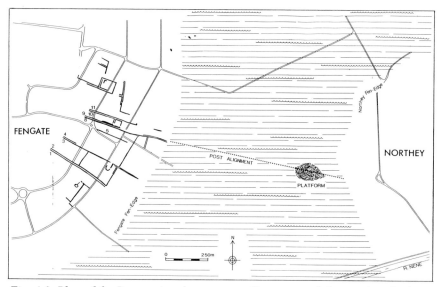

Fig. 4.1 Plan of the Bronze Age droves, post alignment and the wooden platform at Flag Fen (superimposed on modern roads at Fengate and Northey).

The most important site for this period is Flag Fen at Peterborough which has received major excavation and publication (fig. 4.1). The fen itself lies between Fengate, with its complex of earlier yards and droves, and Northey peninsula of Whittlesey island; it is narrow here and contains very substantial archaeological structures. Several rows of large posts cross the fen, linking the drylands, and there is a huge platform built up of many layers and dumps of timber and roundwood, and through which the alignment runs. The platform lies near Northey island. The complex is a later development than the original Fengate system but it is probable that the system was maintained, and enhanced, for some considerable time and thus was the instigation for the eventual development of the alignment and platform. However, the economic system so well demonstrated at Fengate was unlikely to have survived the environmental changes so evident by about 1000 BC, and the alignment and its platform must reflect different and equally demanding perceptions of the Fenland. The post-rows lie just south of the great barrow-field on the Thorney peninsula, which is the watershed between the basins of the Rivers Nene and Welland.

The platform has been examined in part and has yielded many objects, of pottery, stone and metal, as well as quantities of wooden artifacts. No domestic houses seem to have been present, at least in the part so far investigated, and the purpose and activities are not fully understood. Along the alignment, which is about 1000 metres long, were deposited large quantities of metalwork, both tools and weapons (fig. 4.2), as well as bone and other artifacts; most of these were found on the south side. The trees felled to make the two structures indicate a time-range of

Fig. 4.2 Some of the bronze objects found alongside the post rows at Flag Fen.

1363-967 BC, so the activities here were not short-lived. One explanation for the complex involves an economic crisis for the immediate area, when conditions no longer allowed widespread access to increasingly important meadows formerly worked by the Fengate and other communities, with controls for winter grazing and communal meadowland for summer pasture. Perhaps, as conditions deteriorated, the stress on resources necessitated some measure of restricted access to surviving pastures, and a powerful alignment across the fen, reinforced by a large platform, signalled a community in control or trying to assert control. Its own resources were considerable, and over time the alignment was used for some kind of ritualistic behaviour which involved the deliberate destruction and loss of precious objects, ostentatiously deposited in the waters. We still have much to learn about Flag Fen, but already it is clear that the site is one of the most important archaeological monuments in Britain, opening our eyes to information and ideas not otherwise exposed to view.

The deliberate deposition of precious objects in water is a phenomenon known from many other parts of Britain. Often such offerings consisted of single objects, an axe, pot or animal, but on many occasions the gift to the powers was made up

Fig. 4.3 A sheet bronze shield from Coveney Fen, diameter 53 cm.

of groups of objects, bronze weapons and tools, or a pot filled with artifacts. At Wilburton Fen, a large hoard of swords and other bronzes was found in 1882 during peat-cutting; at Stuntney, about 80 axes, sword pieces and ingots were in a wooden tub; at Coveney Fen, two sheet bronze shields were found (fig. 4.3). These and many others from the Fenland may reflect the all-powerful influence of the ever-present waters, and acknowledged since about 4000 BC. The human burials in the fens may have been a part of this ritual – a placatory, dedicatory or commemorative ceremony probably involving many members of the community in an act or acts conducted by the elders to patterns established in times well beyond even their memories.

Settlement of the centuries around 1000 BC is now becoming better known through recent surveys and excavations in the southern Fenland. At Stonea Grange, in Cambridgeshire, a round house and associated ditched fields mark one such occupation, as do cropmarks of rectilinear enclosures near Haddenham. At Cottenham, conditions allowed the partial preservation of a settlement dated to the centuries after 1000 BC. Structural features included fence lines, a building and sheds, ditches and wells, with spreads of occupation debris. One of the wells contained fragments of wooden objects including part of a three-piece wheel made of ash planks held by oak dowels (fig. 4.4). The fen-edge settlement lay in an open

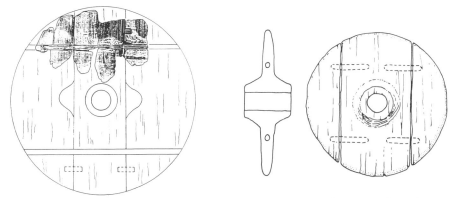

Fig. 4.4 Left, part of a three-piece wheel from a well in a settlement at Cottenham. Diameter 94 cm as reconstructed. Right, a complete tripartite wheel with integral nave and dowels.

landscape with oak and hazel woodland near. Near Ely, an island at Littleport served as a more seasonal camp, amidst the watery fen, and a wooden causeway linked other occupations at Fordey and Little Thetford. The largest hoard of Bronze Age objects ever found in Britain turned up at Isleham in 1960 (fig. 4.5); about 6,500 pieces of metal, weighing 95 kg, included axes, swords, knives, decorative fitments and sheet bronze pieces, as well as casting jets, mould fragments and over 2,600 pieces of slab-cast metal. All of this was encased in a clay-lined pit, deposited prior to re-melting and casting (a founder's hoard) or perhaps intended

Fig. 4.5 A few of the objects from the great hoard of bronzes found at Isleham.
Numbers 1, 3, 7, 10, 11 & 12, decorated mountings including harness fittings:
2, wire drawer: 4, socketed hammer: 5, ferrule for shaft base: 6, cauldron handle:
8, ribbed plating: 9, socketed sickle: 13, small handle.

as a final gift into the fen (a votive hoard). The Fenland at this time must have been a truly formidable place, where nature had asserted itself and overtaken the land, and where previous land-based activities had been extinguished by the inexorable rise of water and water-based sediments. The picture we get from the Fenland at this period in its history is one of a general withdrawal of people from an active participation in the fens, except for a few places where conditions, and personalities, allowed new practices to develop to contend with the new opportunities. And along major parts of the Fenland, people made their own offerings to nature, as their little worlds dissolved.

In the closing centuries BC, the Fenland was increasingly under siege by water. Watertables were higher than ever before, and many low fen islands, occupied by ancestral Neolithic and Bronze Age people, were drowned or much diminished in size. The main rivers followed the same courses as in earlier prehistoric periods, but a band of seaward marine deposits caused an increased expanse of peat-fen against the land (fig. 4.6). The identification of Iron Age settlement in the landscape is relatively recent; as late as 1978 Godwin believed that the Fenland had experienced no Iron Age settlement at all. Early workers attributed this to a widespread flooding that made the region inhospitable. Just as for the Bronze Age, objects of metal (in this case of iron) are not often recovered from Fenland sites, and the term Iron Age is used only as a general chronological guide (about 700 BC to the Roman conquest).

By 700 BC, extensive sea flooding in the central regions was laying down coarse deposits that were to become the silt fen; salt marsh and mudflats encroached over peat and over land that had previously been dry. Brackish water reached the fen-edge along the north-west, backing up brooks and rivers near Billingborough. The southern Fen was an immense expanse of freshwater wetland in which peat formed up to about 2.5 metres above mean sea level. The effect of the drowning can be appreciated by comparing the maps for 300 BC and 1800 BC (fig. 4.6 and fig. 3.1). For instance, the long broad peninsula of Manea, dry in the early prehistoric period, was severed from Stonea in the north and from Coveney in the south, and was itself reduced to three islands. In spite of the general increase of wetness, there was still dry land on the southern islands and promontories. Some settlement sites were located on heavy soils because primitive ploughs (ards) could now cope with clayland. This is the first time that significant settlement remains are found away from light soils.

During the Fenland Survey over 100 sites of Iron Age character were recognised. On the Isle of Ely, for example, only one solitary Iron Age artifact was known before survey began; by the end, seven occupation sites were identified. In Lincolnshire, many settlements and salterns lie on roddons; they mark occupation of the new siltlands for the first time.

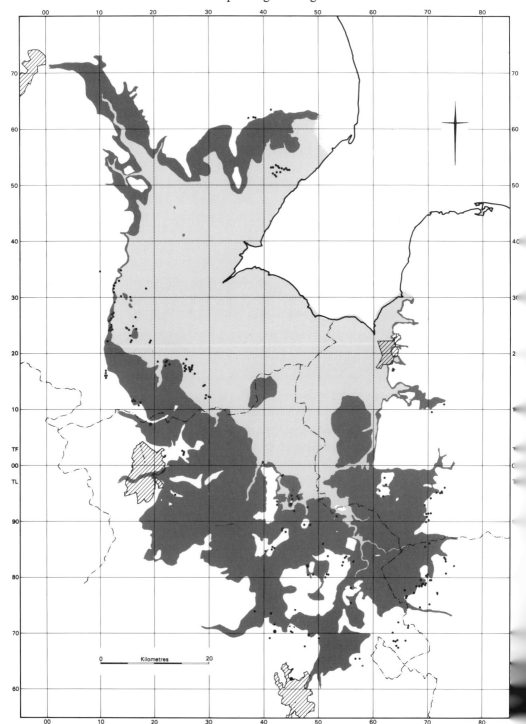

Fig. 4.6 Distribution of Iron Age sites on a map of the fen landscape of about
300 BC. Dark tone peat, light tone silt.

Among the larger sites in the Fenland at this time are several ringworks with earthen ramparts, that elsewhere in the country are called 'hillforts'; in the Fenland they are 'lowforts' in essence. Two scheduled monuments, long known, at Peakirk Moor (Borough Fen) and Willingham, were identified as Iron Age ringworks (fig. 4.7). Another 'camp', at Stonea, was already known as an Iron Age structure.

Fig. 4.7 Enclosure of the Iron Age at Willingham with medieval strip cultivation within and around it. North at the bottom of the photograph.

In Borough Fen, near Peterborough, lies a slightly irregular ringwork with a ditch 220 metres diameter and an inner rampart 1.5 metres high and 4 metres wide (where not destroyed). The main ditch is surrounded by an outer concentric ditch 2 metres wide, which forms a circle of diameter 280 metres. Pottery of about 300 BC was found in the main ditch where it is cut by a roadside dike. The interior of the monument has no visible features being well protected by a covering of alluvium. The ringwork lies on the Iron Age fen-edge and presumably relates to the large number of sites in the Peterborough region.

The Wimblington site of 'Stonea Camp' or the 'Stitches' has long been believed to be an Iron Age ringwork, and was for many years the only identified monument of the period in the Fens. It is a ramparted D-shaped enclosure with more than one bank covering 10 hectares. There were two phases, one 'D' lying inside the other but sharing a common south-west side. Only part of the inner curved ramparts survived recent plough damage; the site has recently been returned to pasture and made open for public interpretation. Excavation of one of the western ramparts showed that it had a single phase of construction without timber supports. Sherds from the excavation and finds of Icenian coins from nearby indicate a date of the middle of the 1st century AD. Four undefended entrances suggest the ringwork was never completed in its latest stage. Other ditches contained a child's skull with sword cuts, complete skeletons of two adults, and other isolated bones. Very few animal bones were found, unlike domestic Iron Age sites, nor were there many finds inside the enclosure. Environmental analysis of the wet deposits found no evidence of agricultural use. The plan is unlike that of most Iron Age enclosures in Cambridgeshire which are generally circular with a single ditch. The closest parallels are found at Thetford, Norfolk, and in Essex, which, with the late date of Stonea, may give credence to the suggestion that it represents expansion of Icenian tribes into the Fenland.

A small ringwork at Wardy Hill, Coveney, enclosing one hectare, was known as a cropmark with an irregular double-ditched enclosure (fig. 4.8). It lies on the Iron Age fen-edge at an estimated 2.7-3.0 metres above mean sea level, surrounded by fen on all sides except the west. On the ground there was an irregular soilmark of ploughed ramparts, 50 metres diameter, still partly earthwork in 1981. The whole area was stained dark and littered with pottery sherds and stones from hearths and yards. Excavation during 1991-2 showed that the principal entrance was defended by a remarkable series of ditches and ramparts, similar to Wessex forts. Inside were four 'huts' with circular eavesdrip gullies that represent successive stages of paired dwellings. Finds were prolific, with 6,000 pottery sherds and 17,000 pieces of bone, even though the site had a short life during the 1st century BC. Environmental evidence indicated that there was arable land nearby and that hedge shrubbery grew along the defensive ramparts. High-status imported pottery of Roman samian and other high quality Continental vessels show that Fenland peoples did not live in isolation from the rest of the country. The ringwork was perhaps the most important of the many Iron Age sites on the Isle of Ely, dominating the small territory and perhaps exerting some form of control over wider areas of the southern Fenland.

In the south-west, Belsars Hill, Willingham, is another impressive circular earthwork, with a high rampart and wide ditch enclosing an area 240 metres diameter, similar to Borough Fen. The site had long been thought to be a Norman ringwork, associated with the siege of Ely, but an Iron Age date is more likely, since the monument interrupts open-field furlongs, strongly suggesting that it predates them. Ridge and furrow within the enclosure does not align with the

Fig. 4.8 Small hillfort at Wardy Hill, Coveney, during excavation. The ditches show as dark lines and the outlines of round houses can be seen.

pattern of the strips outside (shown on an open-field plan of 1812). There is much Iron Age settlement in the vicinity and Belsars Hill is probably best seen as a regional centre.

Other kinds of Iron Age finds and sites are known. In the Witham Valley, at Fiskerton, a timber causeway and many artifacts were discovered in 1979. Trees used in the causeway had been felled over a period of about 75 years (456-375 BC) with a major phase of construction in 406 BC. From the same vicinity in the river valley various swords and a splendid shield of the 2nd century BC have been found (fig. 4.9). The shield consists of a thin bronze sheet facing on a wooden board, and the bosses are of bronze with coral insets. These and many valuable objects from the Witham and the other Fenland rivers may well be offerings to the power of the water and the deities residing within it, thus continuing a tradition already well established at Fengate and Flag Fen. We do not know much about the organisation of the ceremonies that must have accompanied the deliberate loss and destruction of valuable objects; a 'priesthood', songs and chants, a procession, and special food and drink may have been part of the events.

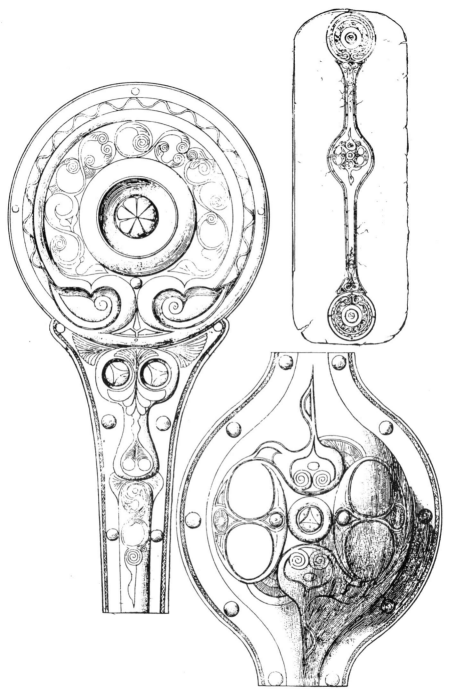

Fig. 4.9 Late Iron Age shield from the River Witham. This is an illustration drawn soon after discovery.

Small scale rural and domestic sites abound on the fen-edge and southern islands. The north-western edge has many Iron Age settlements and salterns, especially near Billingborough and Thurlby. Iron Age structures were discovered at a multiperiod site at Dowsby, where a ring gully had six separate phases of construction. Some fen-edge sites were partly buried and preserved by alluvium and others have cropmarks revealing enclosures and field systems. At Market Deeping, a late Iron Age and Roman site lay beside an ancient channel (fig. 4.10) containing a remarkable deposit of well preserved wood, cobbles, bone and pottery and a rare variety of brooch. Upright timbers with sharpened points probably belonged to a wharf or bridge, and in situ stakes were possibly part of revetments. The pottery has been dated to about 200 BC. There were later Roman enclosures and other features on the site, mostly sealed by alluvium. The Peterborough area, Thorney, Whittlesey, and March and all the southern Fenland islands revealed a large number of Iron Age sites. A large early settlement at Chatteris, covering 10 hectares, yielded environmental evidence for arable cultivation and 13,000 artifacts of pottery, bone and metal when sampled. There were many pits, postholes and segments of annular ditches that represent house sites.

Fig. 4.10 A Late Iron Age channel at Market Deeping, filled with wood, stone, bone and pottery.

Salterns on the Lincolnshire fen-edge, at Bourne, Helpringham and Billingborough, yield briquetage (fragments of fired clay from boiling pans and supports). In the nearby fen, marine roddons with levees were sufficiently dry for limited settlement and suitable for working salt pans. This was the only region with Iron Age settlement out in the fen lying on silt fen mineral deposits. At Cowbit, salterns flourished on the wide levees of the Welland and other major creeks; three groups produced briquetage and domestic pottery of about 300 BC. Spreads of briquetage were generally near 30 metres in diameter; some were slightly mounded, and one appears to remain intact under peaty alluvium. Excavation exposed a saltern hearth surrounded by a circular ditch and fed by other ditches supplying salt water. Much of the site was well preserved under alluvium; a fuller explanation of salterns appears in the next section.

So, in spite of the increased general wetness, the Iron Age period saw a widespread extension of settlement around the fen-edge, on islands and onto the siltlands deposits. Arable cultivation of heavy clay at Coveney and the clayland locations of many settlements illustrate the exploitation of a wider range of soil types than in previous periods. Salt-making made use of fen peat resources. Most of the people were probably part of a hierarchical society in which ringworks and other major structures served to control and direct a variety of communal activities. It is likely that such an organisation was disrupted by the onset of new pressures imposed by Roman domination, although the lives of ordinary people may not have altered much over the centuries.

Chapter 5

Controlling the system

Unlike the period we call the Iron Age, which was barely known in the Fenland before the Survey, monuments of the Roman period have long been recognised. They were described in the 17th century by Dugdale, and afterwards by Stukeley and later workers. Modern research up to 1970 was brought together by the Fenland Research Committee in a volume edited by Charles Phillips. The report encompassed the results of environmental studies, the fieldwork of John Bromwich and Sylvia Hallam, and the evidence of aerial photography, a technique that is very effective on the light soils of the silt fen.

During the Roman period, watertables were generally lower than in the Iron Age, at only 1.5 metres above mean sea level, and there was much settlement on the fen-edge and islands and on the newly deposited marine silts of the central Fenland, near the Wash. The differences in the landscape of the two periods can be seen by comparing figures 4.6 and 5.1. More ground became available for settlement and most of the large rivers maintained their prehistoric positions.

The work of the Fenland Research Committee showed the wealth of Roman activity in the Fenland, and the Fenland Survey mapped yet more sites on the silts, on islands and around the fen-edge. The most remarkable discovery was a large stone building and settlement at Stonea, near March (fig. 5.2). When first identified, in 1979, it appeared as a mound about 73 metres in diameter raised 0.5 metre above the field surface containing building-stone, plaster and ceramic tile debris. Excavations by the British Museum (1980-85) showed that the first phase was a large stone structure, 16 by 16 metres, with an apse on the west side, erected on a stone platform. A hypocaust system heated the building and it had plaster painted like marble, and glazed windows. Its massive footings suggest that it was two or three storeys high, and so would appear as a tower dominating the Fens. It was constructed in the first part of the second century AD, a corridor and hall being added soon afterwards. A similar tower of Roman date survives as a ruin at Anguillara near Rome.

The Stonea site was laid out with a grid of gravel roads forming 'blocks' of urban character, lined with wooden buildings. Both the stone tower and many lesser buildings were demolished in the early 3rd century, but parts of the site were occupied longer. Nearby was a Romano-Celtic temple of square plan, dedicated to Minerva and overlying an earlier shrine. Several cult objects have come from

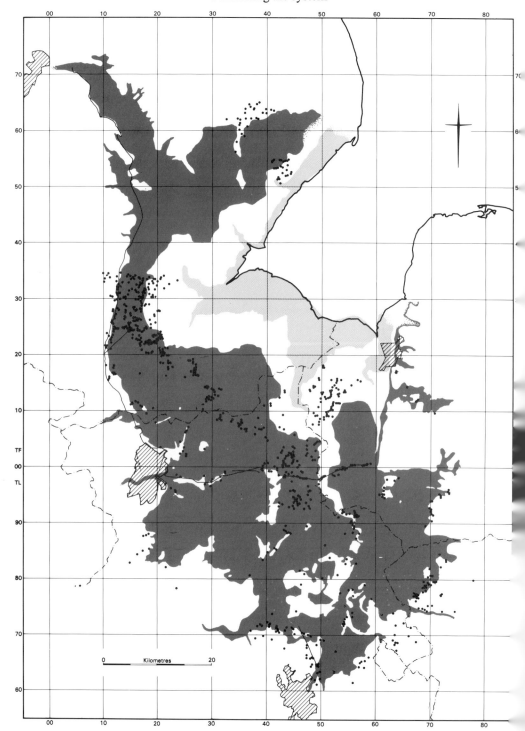

Fig. 5.1 Distribution of Roman sites on a map of the fen landscape of about 200
AD, with major canals. Dark tone peat, light tone silt.

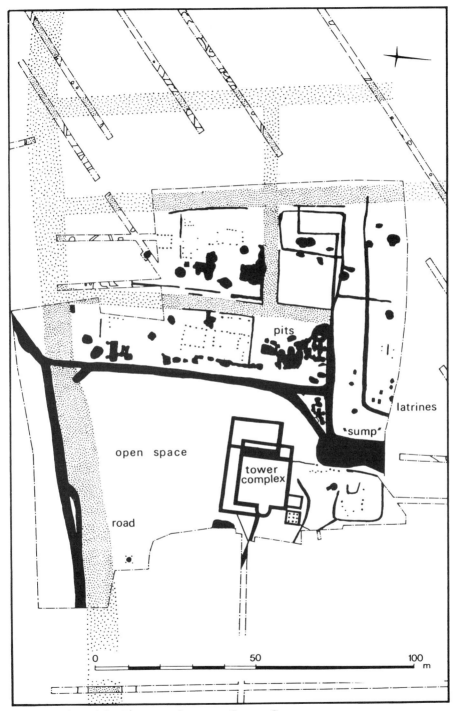

Fig. 5.2 Plan of the Roman settlement at Stonea Grange.

Stonea in recent years, the most striking being a gold votive tablet dedicated to Minerva. There were also a great number of domestic objects (fig. 5.3). The size of the building and the expense involved in assembling its materials (the stone was brought from the Peterborough region, about 30 km away) imply great wealth.

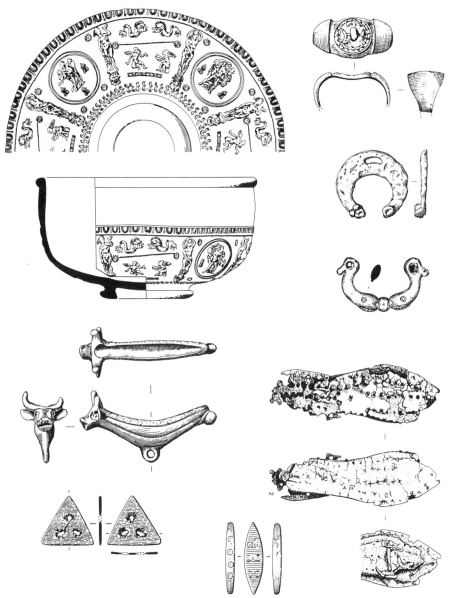

Fig. 5.3 Objects from the settlement at Stonea Grange. Samian bowl (scale 1/4), bronze finger ring (1/1), two handles or mounts (1/2), ox-headed bronze cosmetic grinder (1/2), triangular bone weaving plate (1/2), bone gaming piece (1/2) and pieces of leather shoes (1/6)

It was possibly a political successor of the nearby Iron Age enclosure of Stonea Camp. The site has been interpreted as an administrative and market centre of imperial-owned land.

The large Iron Age settlement at Langwood, Chatteris, also continued into the Roman era. The principal structure was a stone building of three bays, dated to the 2nd or 3rd centuries AD; it had lines of parallel post-holes representing aisles. Again, the site must have been important to attract stone building-material, the only other one known in the southern Fenland. Elsewhere, many Roman villas around the fen-edge are likely to have controlled local sites and territories. In this way the local communities became involved in Roman economic pursuits, and doubtless in supporting regional officials through taxation.

Nearly all Roman Fenland sites were rural and agricultural, especially in the silt fen. Many of them were drowned in the Saxon period, to re-emerge as earthworks unscathed by medieval and later ploughing after Fenland reclamation in the 17th and 18th centuries. Nearly all have been damaged by ploughing during the last 50 years, and there are now only seven surviving as earthworks. The scarcity of Roman earthwork sites in Lowland England gives all the Fenland sites value for their visual appreciation, as well as having potential to provide environmental evidence about the Fenland economy and landscape. Only two places, Holbeach Drove (silt fen) and Cottenham (fen-edge) were previously recognised as significant sites; all are now scheduled monuments. Horbling earthworks are the most extensive in all the Fenland, preserving the centre of a large settlement complex based on three hollow-ways meeting at a T-junction. Networks of enclosures are defined by low banks that mark property boundaries and platforms of house sites (fig. 5.4).

The well known earthwork site at Bullock's Haste, Cottenham, includes the Cambridgeshire Car Dyke and is surrounded by an extensive series of cropmarks. A droveway cuts through two right angles among a network of ditched paddocks. Like Horbling, Bullock's Haste is reminiscent of a medieval deserted village, the drove being a hollow way and the enclosures are defined by ditches that once were probably flanked by hedges. A block of narrow, short ridges lie within one enclosure, each about 20 by 4 metres, formerly interpreted as lazybeds. Recent work in Northamptonshire has shown that beds of this type were vineyards. Many other Fenland sites have cropmarks of similar parallel 'ditches'.

The most interesting Norfolk rural site is to be found at Hilgay, where the earthworks of a small farming settlement are perfectly preserved. They consist of two raised (house) platforms set in rectangular and square enclosures marked by shallow gullies. Two small ringworks lie near the farmstead, 10 and 15 metres diameter, with narrow annular ditches 1 metre wide and flat interiors. The platforms were probably stack-stands, and are the only earthwork examples of the small ring-ditches known as 'fen circle' cropmarks in the silt fens (see below).

Fig. 5.4 Aerial photograph of earthworks at a large Romano-British settlement at Horbling.

Many settlements have produced coin hoards and various items of metalwork over the years. The richest material in the south includes bronze statuettes of Jupiter from Earith (fig. 5.5) found in 1814 and Hercules from Sutton (found before 1891). A rich hoard of votive metalwork discovered in Willingham Fen, in 1857, almost certainly came from a shrine recently identified by aerial photography as a square with internal divisions. Nearby, at Haddenham, a Romano-Celtic shrine was placed upon a Bronze Age barrow, re-establishing the area as a burial and ritual complex; cropmarks revealed an inner and outer rectangular enclosure as well as the barrow ring ditch. Until 1953 rectangular earthworks were visible as banks with external ditches. Excavation in 1983 revealed two phases of shrine activity; the barrow had been deturfed in the mid-2nd century, and a masonry-footed octagonal cell built on its southern edge. In the floor of the octagon were many sheep mandibles with hooves laid out either side, and in two cases a coin had been placed on the teeth. A gravelled and ditched track formed an entrance at the south-east; the whole was enclosed by a rectangular ditch. In the north-west corner of the compound a series of inter-cutting pits contained four complete sheep skeletons, each accompanied by a pot; a boar burial was found at the south-east. The shrine was rebuilt, in the late 3rd century, as a square-post structure on the crown of the barrow mound and

Fig. 5.5 Bronze statue of Jupiter, about 21 cm high, found at Earith.

surrounded by a ring of posts. It is likely that the Haddenham and Willingham shrines served the remarkable concentration of Roman sites lying on the gravel terraces from Over to Waterbeach, along the West Water.

One of the major activities in the silt fen during Roman times was the production of salt. It was obtained by the evaporation of brackish water collected from tidal streams, using peat as fuel. The sites are easily identified on the ground as spreads of poorly fired clay, called briquetage, derived from salt pans and their supports. The fabric is straw-tempered, porous and friable, varying in colour from yellow to brick-red and black. Freshly ploughed-out salterns yield large fragments of supports, usually bricks or cylindrical columns, and occasionally bars similar to those found in pottery kilns. Some pieces of briquetage are accidently green-glazed, through the presence of salt. As in the Iron Age, the distribution of the saltern sites is very much at the fen-edge. Such an arrangement would have the advantage of making it easy to collect brackish water from small brooks as well as allowing each hearth to have its own convenient peat supply.

Salterns have been recognised in Lincolnshire for many years. In Cambridgeshire, although briquetage, 'wattle and daub with clay floors ... in most cases apparently destroyed by fire' and 'firebars' had been found during the 1930s, the saltern industry was not clearly identified in the 1970 publication of Roman sites. Norfolk, too, had no pre-Survey record of salt production. The Survey mapped an industry that proved to be very extensive. In the north, salt production at Wrangle and nearby places continued from the Iron Age. Western Lincolnshire has a marked

Fig. 5.6 Excavation of a saltern at Middleton.

zonal settlement distribution, with a band of sites lying between the fen margin and the peaty, central waterlogged band, almost entirely devoted to salt-making.

Some saltern complexes are very large; Flaggrass, March, has several hectares of briquetage, which in a trial trench was more than two metres thick. Littleport salterns lie in great profusion along the roddon of the Old Croft River. The largest site, at Dairy House Farm, first identified in 1931 when it was an earthwork, covers 3.2 hectares and is a conglomeration of many small subsites with large quantities of briquetage and pottery. In 1931 raised platforms 5-8 metres wide, some of them circular, lay in a network of 'Celtic fields'. The site was ploughed in 1948 revealing 'small brick hearths and clay daub reinforced with straw chaff of wheat'. The interpretation of the platforms as huts may be correct, but equally likely some, if not all, of them were saltern sites, visible in 1988 as concentrations of briquetage.

In Norfolk, some salterns lay near the Wash and are partly buried by later silt deposits, but most lie near the Fen Causeway. Saltern excavations have taken place at Denver and in the Nar valley at Middleton (fig. 5.6). The Middleton saltern was built on a natural mound lying next to a roddon, and had two stages of usage. An annular ditch was linked to feeder channels and had a central clay-lined pit, presumably used as a settling tank. Immediately nearby was a boiling hearth with pedestal-supports for clay evaporation trays. A later production phase was served by a new supply channel leading to hearths and a settling tank on a different part of the site. Briquetage lay in abundance over the whole area.

Salt-making sites are associated with areas of parallel cuts that are interpreted as silt-filled turbaries (fig. 5.7). The largest group occurs at Christchurch, Upwell, covering over 60 hectares. On the ground, ridges of silt lie in groups of parallel banks up to 600 metres in length and about 40 metres apart, consisting of clean pure yellow silt without any trace of artifacts or other remains. Smaller areas show similar patterns of rectangular cuts lying parallel or at right angles to one another. The silt ridges are clearly artificial from their straight parallel lines; as with roddons, the original features were channels (cuttings) that became silted up. Subsequent wastage of peat between them has left the silted channels as ridges. So the effect today is a reversal of what we would normally expect. Previously interpreted as Roman fields or medieval turbaries, a Roman date is proven by the association with salterns. Filling of peat cuttings with mineral deposits would only have occurred in the Roman period, when silt was mobile in natural watercourses. During the Middle Ages extensive turbaries were associated with each village, but, with peat wastage, no trace of them remains on the ground. Several turbary sites modify adjacent watercourses, some having lengths of unnaturally straight or right-angled watercourses nearby. It is possible that water transport was used to move the large quantity of peat needed for the salterns, and for domestic fuel. Similar parallel silt ridges are known in Lincolnshire at Morton, and in Norfolk, where O. G. S. Crawford first photographed them in the early 1930s.

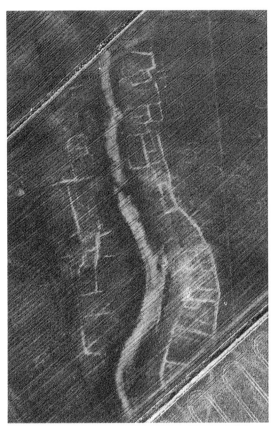

Fig. 5.7
(upper) Aerial photograph of a
Romano-British salt-making
site at Christchurch, Upwell.
(lower) Aerial photograph of
silt-filled turbaries, next to the
above site.

The widespread saltern industry of the siltlands is also closely associated with cropmarks of trackways, paddocks and more extensive planned fields, mainly visible on air photographs. At Christchurch, in Upwell, near the turbaries, lies a remarkable large block of rectangular ditched fields 85 hectares in extent. Like the turbaries, the Christchurch field system reflects a Roman origin by its dimensions, approximately 700 by 1200 metres and equivalent to a Roman measurement of 34 by 20 actus. The actus was the unit most commonly used to mark out a grid of fields (a method known as 'centuriation'). Christchurch fields do not fulfil the requirements necessary for their classification as regular centuriation but may be an example of limitatio, a form of less rigid division used on imperial estates. There are no finds on the ground within the field system, which concords with a pastoral use.

Traces of fields elsewhere in the silt fen rarely show much adherence to a planned axial design. Individual fields are square (or rhomboid) rather than rectangular, another indication that they were used for stock rather than arable. Environmental evidence is required to determine whether the fields had a pastoral regime or whether there was any significant crop production. The silt fen reveals many cropmarks of 'fen circles' or ring ditches about 7-17 metres diameter defined by very fine rings representing ditches of about 0.5 metre width. They are fragile remains, many of them only photographed on a single occasion, suggesting destruction soon afterwards; the minimum number of individual circles in Cambridgeshire is 703.

Only two groups have been recorded as earthworks, at Wisbech St Mary and Hilgay. The Wisbech site was ploughed out in about 1976, but had been previously photographed. It had a series of circular ditches with flat central areas, like the Hilgay earthwork site already mentioned. Many sites have been thoroughly searched on the ground, but no artifacts or soilmarks of any kind have ever been found. A routine agricultural origin is likely, such as drip gullies draining water from thatched roofs of hay or corn stacks. The Christchurch block of Roman fields is associated with many circles, some placed in field corners, suggesting they are of Roman date. Excavation of part of a circle, near the Bourne-Morton canal, indicated an agricultural use because of low phosphate levels and the absence of finds.

Fenland canals older than the 17th century have been recognised for many years, distinguished by having straight lengths, and cutting across bays and natural watercourses. Many of them are late Saxon and medieval works, but some have a Roman origin. The longest and best known structure is the Lincolnshire Car Dyke, running from Peterborough to Lincoln along the fen-edge, a distance of 75 km. It is also the most difficult monument to interpret. Stukeley suggested it was a canal used to transport corn to the northern Roman army. Recent work has challenged this, noting that there are unexcavated crossings and it is not level. However, gaps in canals do not inhibit their function; many 18th-century canals had long breaks until tunnels were made to connect them. Skertchly proposed the Car Dyke as a catchwater, but this implies that it was part of a massive Fenland drainage scheme, and there is no other evidence that the Romans attempted to drain any Fenland.

Another long-distance structure is the Fen Causeway, running across the fen from Denver to Peterborough, described by Dugdale in the 17th century as 'a long causey made of gravel'. It has a complex history, beginning as a canal either side of March island. This seems to have silted up rapidly and two new canals were dug on slightly different alignments from Eldernell to March and across the Norfolk fen. These also silted up and the roddon-like bank was converted to a road by addition of a gravel surface. At Nordelph the causeway is well preserved in a pasture paddock.

The Cambridgeshire Car Dyke links the Cam with the western Ouse, and is different from all other canals in that it cuts through old clays and gravels and not peat fen. There are a variety of other shorter straight channels linking what were active watercourses in the silt fen (as at Tholomas Drove, Wisbech St Mary) or connecting major places with the network (like the Bourne-to-Morton canal) linking the mainland with siltland settlement. A section at Morton showed that it had been 2 metres deep and recut at least once because of silting. Another short canal links Stonea to the Fen Causeway.

The Roman Nene at March was the first Fenland natural river to have a major modification. The prehistoric united Ouse and Nene River running through Wisbech St Mary was replaced with a new channel from Grandford, near March, to Elm. The channel is now a large roddon, and was thought to be natural until a section visible in 1987 revealed the base cutting a metre into underlying gravel, so severing March island. The river is therefore artificial even though it is not straight; farther east it follows a deepened, meandering natural watercourse. The new river explains the great concentration of Roman activity at Elm and emphasises the importance of Grandford as a riverside settlement placed at the Fen Causeway crossing.

All of this evidence shows that the habitable parts of the Roman Fenland were intensively used. Agricultural siltland settlements were mainly concerned with animal rearing and salt production, and were linked to the mainland by canals, tracks and roads. Villas on the fen-edge and the imposing structure at Stonea island probably controlled large territories, as well as having more direct connection with the uplands. What all this meant to the native communities, the farmers, herdsmen and hunters of the Fenland, is not clear, but many people must have been caught up into the wider economic organisation established under Roman rule. When Roman power was withdrawn, in the late 4th century, ordinary lives were probably not affected too much and it was only gradually that changes occurred due to new developments.

Chapter 6

A quiet stability

For several centuries after the end of Roman control shortly after 400 AD, there was little change in the Fenland watertables and a period of stability allowed settlements taken over by the Saxons to continue to grow, augmented with sites in new locations. The fen-edge and the higher spots on the siltlands were preferred locations for occupation, but later, conditions began to deteriorate, and by 700 AD profound changes had taken place, with an increase of wetness that must have been catastrophic to the well-established communities. There was widespread deterioration with inundations by the sea and by inland waters so forming the extensive fen described by monastic writers of the 12th century.

Evidence for the presence of the Saxons falls into three types; settlements identified archaeologically by pottery and domestic refuse, either as surface field-scatters or observed during ground disturbance in existing villages; early pagan cemeteries with grave goods; and the written record of chronicles and charters supplemented by place-names. Until relatively recently only the last two types of evidence were available, very few Saxon settlement sites older than 850 AD being identified before 1960.

The Saxon period is conventionally divided into three phases (Early, Middle and Late), dated approximately to the years 400-650, 650-850, and 850-1066 AD. These three periods correspond approximately to the pagan period, the early Christian era, and the period when present-day villages were founded. Settlements are dated by pottery types. Early pottery is hand-made, often having a dark, hard fabric filled with sand or igneous rock-fragments that glisten in sunlight. A small proportion of early vessels had stamped and linear decoration (fig. 6.1), especially cremation urns found in pagan cemeteries. Local pottery of the Middle Saxon period is similar to that of the early phase, and cannot always be distinguished from it; there is a trend towards thinner sherds and decoration is rare. In East Anglia, a distinctive and mass-produced pottery, called Ipswich Ware, was commonly used in the Middle Saxon period from the 7th to the 9th century. It is wheel made, with a predominantly grey colour and differentiates the Middle from the Early Saxon period. Ipswich Ware is found in the fen and on fen-edge sites. Wheel-made Late Saxon pottery, known as St Neots, Stamford and Thetford Wares, is easily distinguished from material of the earlier periods by its superior technology. Sherds of these wares are found throughout the region.

Fig. 6.1 Early Saxon pottery from Cambridge.

The Saxons did not arrive in an empty Fenland, but found the busy Roman countryside that we have described previously. As might be expected, they settled at some of the Roman sites. Early Saxon occupation debris was found at the large site at Stonea Grange, where there were post-holes and slots representing timber buildings. This parallels discoveries of Early Saxon material found at most Roman villa sites on upland Cambridgeshire, Northamptonshire and elsewhere in the East Midlands. Fenland Roman sites of much lower status than Stonea also produce Saxon pottery. Four of the eight sites newly discovered at the northern fen-edge, near West Keal and Stickford, Lincolnshire, continued from the Roman period. Stickford was a frontier settlement on the southern periphery of the kingdom of Lindsey. It occupied a strategic position that could control movements along the Stickney ridge, the main access into the northern Fenland. Within the Fenland proper, Saxon sherds occur at the siltland sites of Gosberton and Pinchbeck.

Many Saxon sites lie on river gravels, as found elsewhere in the country, both Early and Middle Saxon occurring on the south-west Lincolnshire fen-edge, from Sempringham to Thurlby, some continuing from the Roman period. Several pottery concentrations are known on the Welland Valley terraces. Middle Saxon material, dated by Ipswich Ware pottery sherds, has come from Ely. Otherwise the islands of the southern fen have produced few Early or Middle Saxon finds, it being likely that most early sites are concealed by the existing villages. On the southern fen-edge gravels, several settlements were discovered during the Fenland Survey. One, at Waterbeach, produced sherds and domestic bone in discrete concentrations that may represent houses; a fine piece of gilt bronze metalwork with a zoomorphic decoration was probably once part of a casket or brooch.

A house excavated on the edge of the Car Dyke at Waterbeach, in 1927, revealed a sunken floor level, 0.6 metre below the outside ground surface. It was covered by a black fill containing a dog skeleton and plain hand-made pottery sherds. Decorated sherds were found similar to types used as cinerary urns. Such sunken-floor buildings are frequently found at Early Saxon sites and debate continues whether they were houses or workshops. Sites recently tested or excavated in advance of development at nearby villages have produced more Early Saxon finds, and substantial sites have been found in the village centres of Cottenham and Willingham. All three periods of Saxon remains were found at Snailwell within the medieval village area and, in Suffolk, at Lakenheath two settlement sites are known, one early. Off the eastern fen-edge, at West Stow, Suffolk, Saxon houses have been reconstructed from the evidence of the nearby excavated remains. Along the Nar Valley, Norfolk, Early Saxon sherds were found at a large Roman site at Pentney and Ipswich Ware came from Shouldham.

Pagan cemeteries with grave goods are found all around the fen-edge and on some of the Cambridgeshire islands. In Lincolnshire an early cemetery at West Keal was in use before 500 AD, with possible Anglian or Anglo-Frisian connections. Another early cemetery at Baston dates from the mid-5th to late 6th centuries AD. In western Cambridgeshire cemeteries were found at Eye, Whittlesey, and in the Isle of Ely. Two Saxon cemeteries are known in Ely parish. One, revealed when Witchford aerodrome was levelled in 1947, exposed about 30 skeletons, some with grave goods including iron and bronze buckles, an iron sword, amber beads, various brooches and two fragmentary spearheads (fig. 6.2), dated to the 5th-7th centuries. A pendant made of crystal, gold, coloured glass and precious stones, of the 8th century, was ploughed out nearby in 1952; it had Christian motifs and probably belonged to a royal personage. Recently, at Haddenham, skeletons and 6th-century grave goods were discovered in the village. Saxon burials at Snailwell have been found with weapons and silver rings, and a spearhead was recovered from the excavations of a nearby barrow in 1939. Cemeteries are known from Lakenheath and Mildenhall.

On the siltlands, previous work had shown the presence of a few Middle Saxon sites from the Spalding region and many more were discovered during the Fenland Survey. New sites were placed precariously on roddons open to tidal influence, many being abandoned by the end of the 9th century as a rising watertable approached its high medieval level. A dispersed settlement pattern occurs with many sites lying away from the centres of medieval and modern villages. Two sites were found on the small siltland area of Cambridgeshire, at Tydd St Giles, each producing a finely tooled whetstone with a perforation, presumably intended for suspension from a belt. A brooch and cremation urns of pagan date were found at Wisbech. Geophysical survey over a pottery scatter at a Gosberton Middle Saxon site identified pits and ditches subsequently revealed by excavation. The earliest

Objects of the Pagan Saxon Period
from 'Cratendune', nʳ Ely (Ely Fields Fm.)
48.2265-7 & 48.2451-5. C.A.S. XLI. p.72.

Fig. 6.2 Saxon metalwork from a cemetery near Ely.

structures were deep, wet pits used for hemp retting, yielding a 7th-8th century comb. Later linear ditches were filled with ash and subtidal marine flooding layers. The latest features were beam slots of rectangular buildings and circular gullies, one recut many times. Arable crops were mainly barley with some wheat, rye, oats, peas and flax. Bones of horse, cattle, sheep, poultry and fish were found.

In Norfolk Marshland, six sites were spaced regularly on roddons between West Walton and Terrington St Clement. Excavation at three of them revealed pits and buried ditches, but no domestic structures. Little metalwork was found, implying that the settlements were of low status. Norfolk Middle Saxon sites were open to the sea and exposed to fast moving tidal water. Environmental remains of seeds, pollen and bone showed, surprisingly, that limited arable agriculture was possible under these conditions, making use of salt-tolerant barley. Presumably the highest ground on the backs of roddons was utilised.

The landscape during the Early Saxon era is illustrated in figure 6.3. All sites visited and newly discovered during the Fenland Survey and the locations of some

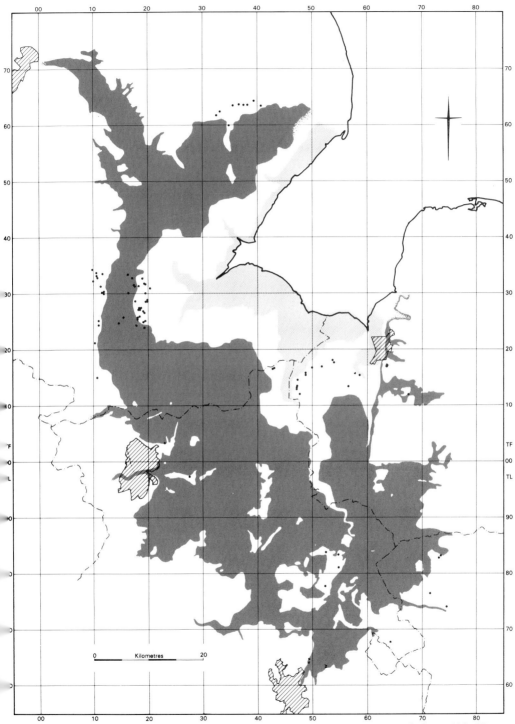

Fig. 6.3 Distribution of Saxon sites on a map of the fen landscape of about 600 AD. Dark tone peat, light tone silt.

of the cemeteries known from earlier finds are marked. The distribution is markedly on river and fen-edge gravel with some in the silt fen.

Historical evidence, mainly for the Late Saxon period, comes from place-names, charters and the chronicles of the great Fenland Saxon monasteries. In Linconshire, the place-names Billingborough and Billinghay, villages located on the fen-edge some 20 km apart, may derive from the Bilmigas, a people referred to in the tribal hidage of about 700 AD. All the region was perhaps the territory of this Saxon tribe. The name Rippingale, recorded in 806, is of Saxon origin, and probably relates to the Hrepingas of 675 AD, a group of Middle Anglians who settled in the general vicinity of Rippingale village. The Marshland place-names Walpole, Walsoken and Walton, recorded in the 10th and 11th centuries, incorporate the Anglo-Saxon element w(e)alh meaning a 'Briton' or 'Welshman', which accords with the dense Roman settlement of the area. The earliest surviving charter for Norfolk, 942, describes a grant by King Edmund of a substantial area in Southery to Theodred, bishop of London.

Fig. 6.4 The Sea Bank near Wisbech viewed from the western, landward, side.

Around the whole of the Wash there was a protective earthen barrier called the Sea Bank or Sea Dyke, built to prevent marine flooding (fig. 6.4). It extended along tidal parts of the major rivers at Elm and in Marshland. Antiquarians of the 17th century referred to the Sea Bank as a Roman structure, but the term 'Roman Bank' was not recorded before then, and there is no evidence for a Roman origin. The first record of the name is in 1178 when it was already esteemed to be 'old'. A Middle Saxon site at Tilney St Lawrence, set on a low levee beside the river Ouse, is partly covered by the Bank which is therefore of later date. Middle Saxon sites at Walpole St Peter similarly have occupation debris running up to the Sea Bank and may continue underneath. The proximity of the earliest siltland villages to the Bank suggests that it was in existence by the Late Saxon period, to protect arable fields. The banks were previously believed to be pre-1066 from the evidence of settlements and fields already well established by the early 12th century.

Recent excavations at Terrington St Clement and West Walton Saxon sites showed conclusively that the Sea Bank was in existence in the Late Saxon period. Pits and ditches were filled with domestic refuse without any accumulation of high energy tidal silts, unlike the Middle Saxon phase. There must have been protection by the Sea Bank to stop the tidal deposits so effectively. A partial section of the Bank at Clenchwarton showed it had been built directly on mudflats, with no development of topsoil, as would be expected if it were built in marginal conditions with a rising sea level threatening habitation.

The Sea Bank is a major flood defence for the settlements and fields of the whole siltland. It relates to other major fen banks, to river embankments and river diversions, that are all likely to be Late Saxon works. When the Sea Bank was needed, there would have to be banks against the fen as well, for the fen watertable would rise with the sea. Having undertaken such large-scale flood defence works it became desirable to rationalise and divert the channels of the sluggish brooks and rivers flowing along their prehistoric courses in roddons. The whole of the earliest stage of the siltland landscape thus became established; the core of vills, the small irregular fields, and the inner fenbanks shown on the 'medieval' plans (see fig. 7.5), almost certainly have a Late Saxon origin.

The effectiveness and necessity for the Sea Bank is evident at Walpole St Andrew and Leverington, where silt on the seaward side of the earthwork lies two metres higher than the level of the protected agricultural land. The Bank was increased in size over the years as demanded by the rising sea-level. Gordon Fowler inspected a new cut through the Cambridgeshire Sea Bank in Leverington and noted that the earliest phase was only one metre high and it had been subsequently made up by three separate additions. As late as 1617, the banks were described as being 'heretofore made for the defendinge of the landes from the force and rage of the sea'.

Chapter 7

Chronicled lives

The Fenland story from the Middle Ages begins with the Norman Conquest of 1066. We have a graphic account of conditions at this time. In about 1150 a monk of Peterborough Abbey wrote:

...floods and overflowing rivers cause the water to stand on all the land forming a deep marsh which is uninhabitable, except at certain places...Within the marsh, it is not possible to go to Ramsey, Thorney, Crowland and elsewhere, unless by boat, (except, with difficulty, on one side of Ramsey). Ely is an island in the same territory, being seven miles long and the same broad, containing 22 villages, surrounded by marsh and water, but it has the benefit of three causeways. At Burgh [Peterborough]... the same marsh begins on the east side, and continues for 60 miles and more. However, the fen is at the same time useful for men; from it they obtain wood and rushes for fires; hay and fodder for draught beast, and thatching for house roofs and many other uses. There are fruitful rivers and remote fisheries. Truly, there are diverse streams and many waters and great pools well stocked with fish; the whole region has an abundance of these things.

The wetlands consisted of peat; there were no active marine phases because seabanks provided protection around the Wash. This enabled the siltlands, partly settled by the Saxons, to be developed fully. The urban centres at Lincoln, Peterborough and Cambridge, established in Roman times, continued as places of regional significance. Siltland ports at Boston, Spalding, Wisbech and King's Lynn were also important. In the south, peninsulas and large islands supported substantial villages, especially on the Isle of Ely.

The cathedral at Lincoln and the major Saxon monasteries at Ely and Peterborough influenced the medieval organisation. Ely was the dominant centre in the south, being elevated to a cathedral city in 1109; it possessed almost the whole of the Cambridgeshire Fenland and many estates beyond. There were further significant local centres at the Saxon monasteries of Crowland, Thorney and Ramsey, but they never developed urban status, even though their possessions were considerable (fig 7.1). Smaller religious houses, granges and hermitages, often placed in isolated spots (fig. 7.2), added to a settlement pattern already fragmented by peninsulas and islands. Few of the religious sites, apart from the cathedrals, have any upstanding remains. Crowland abbey church is an imposing landmark in the level landscape but all that is left of Thorney abbey, founded in 972, is part of the 12th-century nave used as the parish church.

Fig. 7.1 St Vincent's Cross marking the boundary between the estates of Crowland, Thorney and Peterborough monasteries.

Fig. 7.2 Earthworks of a monastic grange at Rigbolt, Gosberton.

Many large manors had parks, such as the Peterborough abbey manor of Eyebury, and the Ely manor at Little Downham. A park and palace, first recorded in 1222, was frequented by medieval bishops of Ely, five of whom died at Downham. The park has a distinctive boundary, forming a large oval enclosure. Ely demanded two deer annually from Downham Park; in 1222 and 1251 customary dues from Littleport tenants included enclosing the Park with a ditch.

Fen-edge settlements often had long tongues of land extending into the fen to take advantage of the wetland resources and parishes. This is very marked on the south-west Lincolnshire fen-edge, Billingborough and Hacconby being 8 km long from upland to fen but they are only 2 km and 1 km wide respectively.

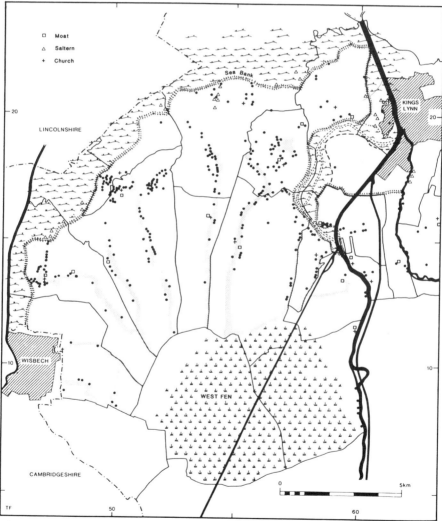

Fig. 7.3 Marshland Drove settlement with many small sites along wide tracks leading to the fen.

As with the Roman and Saxon periods, the silt fen is a distinctive area, very different from the fen-edge or the islands of the south. Even now, it is notable for attractive stone-built medieval churches, early brick houses, and many trees near the villages. The whole area is a remarkably unchanged medieval landscape in its general layout. The settlement pattern is dispersed, for, although the oldest villages lie spaced out on the highest ground near what was the Wash coast line, reclamation and extension of the fields into the fen encouraged the spread of new hamlets and linear settlements along wide access droves. Marshland, Norfolk, is the most striking example of drove development, where seven droves link the main villages to a large common marsh lying 5 km to the south (fig. 7.3). Archaeological finds confirm this growth; 240 medieval pottery spreads from Marshland yielded 33,570 sherds, mapping the settlement expansion, there being a great increase in the 13th century. The droves are well illustrated by Haiwarde's late-16th century map of Marshland. One of the best preserved is at Tilney St Lawrence, where the 14th-century parish church lies on one side and the manorial site of Aylmer Hall sits opposite, 120 metres away, giving an immediate appreciation of the drove width. The drove edges are accentuated by the earthworks of medieval houses or existing dwellings.

The western fen-edge and all the islands had fields ploughed in narrow, ridged strips of Midland type, grouped in blocks called furlongs. East of Cambridge and on the East Anglian fen-edge there was similar strip cultivation but with slight or no ridging. Most individual ridges are now ploughed out, but furlong boundaries survive as long soil banks in modern arable fields, and can be mapped to reconstruct complete open-field patterns. Many places have maps and surveys of their fields, such as Toynton (1614) and Chippenham (1712). Willingham has a field survey of 1812, arranged in groups of furlongs, each of which has a map, one showing the Iron Age ringwork, Belsars Camp (see fig. 4.7). The open-field 'home farms' (demesnes) of Ely monastic properties are fully described in surveys made in 1222 and 1251. In 1222, Haddenham demesne had 919 acres of strips divided nearly equally between three fields. The surviving furlong boundaries correspond well with a map dated 1827. Soham has never been enclosed and the modern landscape is that of the Middle Ages, especially in No Ditch Field and in North Field where the main boundaries of present-day farms lie between linear furlong boundaries (fig 7.4). Two commons belong to the open-field land, called North Horse Fen and South Horse Fen, which lie unploughed with an uneven surface, pocked by large anthills.

Medieval arable land in the siltland was divided into strip fields as well, but the parcels were bounded by dikes and not ridged up. Strip widths commonly varied from 12 to 20 metres. Fields near the original villages have short strips, but in reclaimed areas massive fields were laid out with strips up to 1.5 km in length. In most cases a 'field' consists of a single group of strips lying in the same orientation, corresponding to a Midland 'furlong', but much larger in area; the strips were called dylings or darlands. Quadring has some of the few strip-fields surviving in

Fig. 7.4 Aerial photograph of the open fields of Soham.

earthwork form (now protected as a Scheduled Monument). The complete field systems of Cambridgeshire and Norfolk siltland have been reconstructed from historical sources (fig. 7.5). Large-scale fen reclamation took place, beginning in the Late Saxon period and continuing throughout the Middle Ages in some parts of the siltland. These large intakes give rise to long straight lines of fields and droves, especially in the southern Lincolnshire siltland, where they stretch for 8 km.

The fen, although often depicted as a dreary wasteland in contemporary descriptions, was a valuable resource of food, fuel, and grazing. Complex agreements existed between manors about rights of usage. Ramsey and Thorney abbeys had claims in Ramsey marsh and it was agreed, in 1224, that Thorney should have that part lying towards its manors of Yaxley and Farcet. Peat was dug extensively; in 1125 work-services due to Peterborough Abbey included cutting a cart load of reeds from Thurlby. Little Downham villeins could cut turves in 1325, valued one shilling per 500, but not sell them to the men of other villages. Sedge,

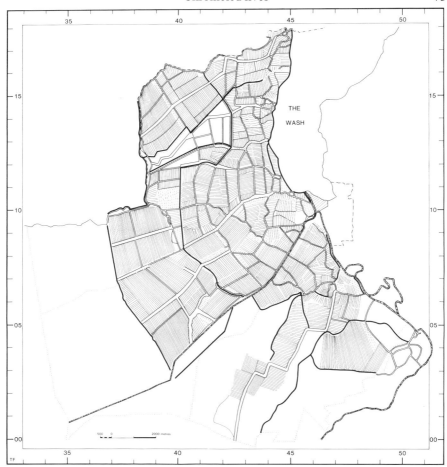

THE

WASH

TF

Fig. 7.5 Fields in the Cambridgeshire silt fen. Thick lines represent earthen banks built to prevent flooding of the land.

used for thatching, was likewise freely available to the villagers, but was not to be sold beyond the bounds of Downham in 1315. Manorial officers were appointed to keep the fen under control, and in the summer this included ensuring that it did not catch fire, as happened in 1376. Peat from turbaries was claimed by several Norfolk religious houses, some of them far from the fen, such as Castle Acre and Wendling.

The only industries of the Fenland, apart from the direct exploitation of its natural resources, were production of salt and pottery, both fuelled by peat. Pottery was made in many centres around the Fenland, including Toynton All Saints, Bourne, King's Lynn and Grimston. Recently kiln sites have been found at Ely and Colne. By the 16th century, brick-making was a significant activity around Ely, with kilns at Shippea and Little Downham.

Fisheries were valued possessions and rents were sometimes paid in eels. We have noted the 12th-century description by the Peterborough monk of marshes teeming with fish. Any pool or length of water was potentially a fishery in a practical or legal sense. Particular places were sometimes used regularly for fishing and these can be identified on the ground as small spreads of sherds, bones, and lead fish-line weights. Fisheries were recorded in a 1115 grant to Bardney Abbey, and small 13th-century sites at East Kirkby yield pieces of 'curfew' pottery (for carrying fire embers) and were probably fish-smoking sites. The River Witham has produced several large stone fish-net weights. Whittlesey Mere was famous for its fishing; landing stages were mentioned in a boundary description of the Mere made in 1225-28. In 1306 the abbot of Thorney had five 'cotes' abutting on the Mere and five boats were allowed to fish. Several cotes are marked on a map of 1786, and during the recent survey three sites were discovered on the south side of the Mere. One produced sherds of 13th-century and later pottery and large numbers of lead fish-line weights. Excavation evidence showed that small fish were being used as bait for pike and other large species.

Salt was made in the silt fen from wind dried, salt encrusted coastal mud. Extraction of concentrated brine and evaporation of the solution using peat fuel yielded solid salt. High mounds or banks of waste mud were formed as a result of this process. On the northern coast, salt-making is recorded in the 11th century at Friskney and Wainfleet, where large mounds can be seen. Bicker Haven salt industry is referred to in the 1086 Domesday Survey and even today there are spectacular mounds rising to three metres. A levelled mound revealed two peat-fired hearths with 14th-century pottery; briquetage was not found, showing that salt extraction methods differed from those of the Iron Age and Roman periods. Within the Haven are pits, presumably used as settling tanks, associated with the name Saltcote Floors (fig. 7.6). Large quantities of peat were required to support the salt boiling, hence a grant to Waltham Abbey, in the late 12th century, gave pasturage in Wrangle for oxen 'sufficient to maintain seven salterns at the rate of six oxen to each saltern'.

It is probable that the large banks on the seaward side of the Sea Bank at Newton, Cambridgeshire, previously interpreted as breakwaters, are saltern mounds. They are similar to the mounds found at Bicker Haven and West Walton, but those at Newton form long banks in the estuary, acting as breakwaters. Unique to Cambridgeshire are small medieval salterns placed on roddons in the peat fen near Tydd St Giles. All produce much pottery of 13th and 14th-century date, with hard, bright-red fragments of brick. The 'briquetage' would indicate that the sites were salterns, being exactly paralleled by Roman salterns, exploiting tidal brooks flowing down the middle of roddons. Excavation at Parson Drove revealed settling tanks and channels supplying salt water. Bricks were used to construct hearths and the evaporating vessels were probably large pottery jars.

Fig. 7.6 Settling tanks for salt extraction at Bicker Haven.

In Norfolk Marshland, salt making left tell-tale groups of mounds beside the Sea Bank. Domesday Book records salterns attached to several holdings in Lynn in 1086 and these continued well into the Middle Ages. Abutting the outer face of the Sea Bank near Ingleborough are large mounds, up to 200 metres long and 3 metres high, described as the 'Salt Hills' on a map of about 1600.

By the Middle Ages many changes in the courses of rivers and brooks were necessary to improve summer grazing and to protect the rich agricutural siltland. The process had begun in the late Saxon period with the formation of the first sea banks and the necessary control of fresh-water outflows. Silts blocked the prehistoric River Witham and the present course, close to the eastern edge of the valley, was used by 1331 and probably as early as 1086. South of Dogdyke, the transfer of the main outfall from Bicker Haven to Boston took place before 1205, when there was much river traffic along the Witham between Boston and Lincoln. Some of the Nene water was taken by a canalised version of its natural course, the Whittlesey Dyke, directly from Peterborough to Benwick. Other Nene water found a circuitous course through Whittlesey and Ramsey Meres to Benwick.

The River Ouse ran from Earith west of the Isle of Ely, joined with the Nene at Benwick, and continued to Wisbech through March. An artificial channel, 12 km long, cut through a narrow neck of land in March island extending to the Old

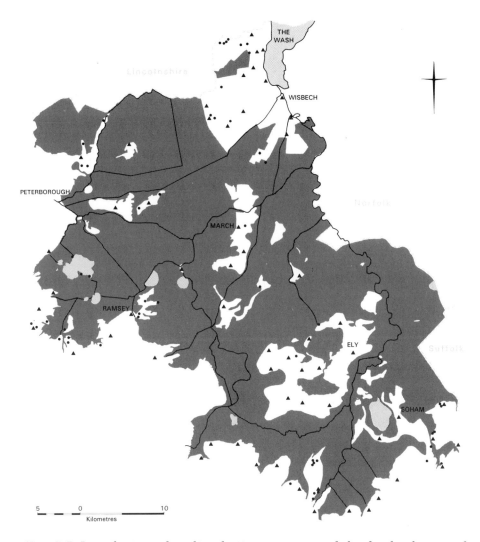

Fig. 7.7 Distribution of medieval sites on a map of the fen landscape of Cambridgeshire, about 1500 AD. Dark tone peat, light tone meres. Triangles major settlements, circles minor settlements.

Croft River at Upwell. This large drainage work, a replacement of the Roman one to Elm, was probably made in the Late Saxon period, to help the drainage of the siltlands. By the early Middle Ages some of the Ouse waters flowed from Earith, south of the Isle of Ely, and joined the Cam. The eastern Ouse-Cam had a sinuous course between the Ely islands of Stuntney and Quanea, but by the 12th century a diversion was made to Ely, doubtless for the benefit of the monastery and cathedral. The river once ran to Wisbech, but another straight length of the Ouse, the Ten Mile River, probably made at the same time, took all the south-eastern Fenland waters to Downham Market and King's Lynn. The main drains of the silt fen are almost entirely artificial, even though some of them are far from straight.

As well as the major rivers and drains there was a complicated network of local brooks and canals, called lodes, linking the rivers to form a communication network between fen-edge vills and the islands. Many fen-edge brooks were taken to major drains by canals, such as the lodes of Billingborough, Pointon, and Hacconby, which fed into the midfendik, cut along the centre of a peat belt between the siltlands and the western Lincolnshire upland. The lodes of Swaffham and Reach had quays at the villages.

Many lodes are obvious artificial canals, cutting straight across the fen, like those belonging to the abbeys at Ramsey and Sawtry, used to bring building stone from the Peterborough region. In 1230 it is recorded that Monkslode, at Sawtry, had been made 'to preserve the lands, meadows and pastures of the men of Walton, Sawtry and Conington from the waters descending...and for navigation of corn, turves and other things to diverse places'. Some crooked lodes were also canals. The Darcey Lode, west of Manea, followed the contour of the medieval fen-edge on the west and then utilised a natural watercourse along a roddon. It continued south as the Oxlode, taking a straight course to Little Downham Hithe (fig. 7.7).

The name hithe, meaning port or quay, is common around the southern fen. Near Downham Hithe quantities of fine pottery, whetstones and pieces of lava quernstone were found, the debris of Fenland imported cargoes. Ely expanded down to the edge of the diverted river Ouse, and several hithes were constructed. Bradehide was mentioned in 1210, and nearby were castel hythe, monkeshithe and stokhithe. A hithe at Setchey on the River Nar was ordered to be cleansed of wrecks, rubbish and silt in 1274-5. Yaxley, lying far from the sea, was a significant inland port throughout the Middle Ages; coal and other goods were transported inland 55 km to central Northamptonshire as late as 1628.

In the southern Fenland, dominant features of the landscape were freshwater lakes called meres. Whittlesey Mere, in the west, was one of the largest lakes in the country, at about 760 hectares. It formed part of the Fenland transport network, and, when drained in 1848-52, large pieces of stone were found, a capsized cargo once destined for a monastic house or church. The meres are now marked by spreads of white marl. Soham Mere was sufficiently large, at 500 hectares, to give its name 'Sea-ham' to the village.

Land reclamation in the peat fen was very limited; it was not possible to keep water out of the lows created by peat shrinkage until pumps were available. The largest intake was in Coveney fen, called the Dams, enclosed before 1636. It was subdivided by irregular linear dikes into long narrow enclosures.

The silt fen continued to be defended from sea flooding by the Sea Bank, and fresh water from the fen was controlled by several Fen Banks. The enclosed land was drained by means of sluices, called gotes where main brooks ran through the Sea Bank. At low tide they were left open to remove fresh water from the embanked area and closed at high tide to keep out the sea. An interesting sluice at Newton near Wisbech, representing a minor drain, was discovered in 1976. A 10 metre length was exposed, constructed of three hollowed-out tree trunks, one metre diameter, tapered at the ends to fit into each other. They were laid on sleeper beams, to prevent sinking, and further stabilised with uprights fixed to more beams on top of the trunks and the whole covered with planks.

The original core of Saxon drained land, protected by sea banks and fen banks, was extended, mainly by taking in fen, sometimes on a large scale. At Elloe Wapentake major fen banks ran 22 km across several parishes, suggesting co-operative construction. Norfolk has a complex succession of fen banks encroaching on Marshland. The Cambridgeshire siltlands had a simpler reclamation history. An inner fen bank marks the first stage and a single outer fen bank encloses two separate large intakes probably of 12th-century date; the largest intake was 2,430 hectares (fig. 7.5).

Although there were protective seabanks, serious floods occurred. The village of South Clenchwarton, recorded in 1277, had a chapel in 1334; it was destroyed and of no value because of sea flooding in 1369. In 1907 two coffin lids were found on the river bank, and a scatter of chalk building fragments was all that remained in 1984. The Clenchwarton flood, in overall Fenland terms, may have been but a minor inconvenience, just one of a multitude of such events, but it illustrates the persistent threat of inundation, sometimes sudden, and of course the effect on individual lives was severe. The later history of the Fenland reflects awareness of the potential dangers, by the communal efforts to embank and drain and protect major parts of the Fenland. Small groups could do little; it required major organisation and resources, initiated by the Romans in their marketing and transportation schemes, continued by the Saxons in the first real attempts to drain the land, and consolidated by medieval towns and monastic centres which combined their commercial interests with reclamation of land and protection of the resources.

Chapter 8

Draining the past and preserving the future

In spite of the protective banks and complex drainage channels of the silt fen, the Fenland was always under threat. All the waters of the East Midlands and south had to find a way across the fen to the sea. The peat fen hustled against the fen banks, rising 1.5 metres higher than the silt, and the sea sometimes flowed over breaches in sea banks. Protection of Ely's monastic estates in the Wisbech region was the likely reason for the Nene diversion at March in the 10th century, and again, more than 500 years later, the silt fen was still threatened by the wide expanse of soggy peat to the west and south. A long, almost straight channel, later called Morton's Leam, was dug from Peterborough directly to Guyhirn in 1478, outfalling into the Saxon and medieval Great River of Wisbech. This relieved the southern peatlands by reducing the amount of water flowing along the two southern courses of the Nene.

Commissions of Sewers were appointed by the crown to improve drainage in the late Middle Ages. Local courts determined what should be done; some of the proceedings have been published by Dugdale. Dissolution of the monasteries in 1539 caused dispersion of estates and fragmented the responsibility for drainage works. This caused neglect of essential maintenance and in the 1570s floods drowned 16,000 acres (6,500 hectares) of land. The first general drainage scheme, made in 1593, proposed cutting new straight channels. Many more schemes were considered in the early 17th century but there was also opposition. Many fenmen thought that nature should be left alone, and there would be interference with navigation, devaluation of pasturage and loss of common rights. There was also objection to the use of foreign labourers.

In the southern Fenland, known as the Great Level (until 1663, when it was called the Bedford Level), Francis, earl of Bedford, undertook a scheme to drain the peatlands in 1631 appointing the Dutchman Cornelius Vermuyden as engineer. The earl was to receive 95,000 acres (38,500 hectares) of drained fen, the rent of 40,000 acres (16,000 hectares) to be used for maintenance works. Vermuyden was a determined and controversial person, opposed by fenmen and others; he created a system of new straight drains to take water directly across the fen from the main rivers, following Dutch methods. Many thought it would have been better to put a series of new cuts into existing rivers so increasing the volume of water which would help keep them naturally scoured out. The system devised gave problems, silt collecting at the major river outfalls 'and to the end of time must continue to do so'. The object of the 'undertaking' was to make the Level 'summer land', that is ground dry in the summer but liable to flood in winter, like upland river meadows. Although the task was declared complete in 1637 it was adjudged to be defective in 1638.

The northern peat Fenlands had similar, but smaller, schemes. Deeping Fen was drained in 1637, and in the Lindsey Level, Holland Fen was drained in 1638 when South Forty Foot drain was dug. The East Fen near Stickney received attention in 1631-34, but banks were destroyed during the Civil War and not made good until the 18th century. Further work in the Great Level was in abeyance during the Civil War, but an Act of 1649 was passed to make the Level 'winter ground' (flood-free all the year round) by 1656, except for the meres. In 1650 a petition against the works was made by Cambridge University because of interference with direct navigation from King's Lynn. Eventually Cam water traffic ceased and goods came no longer via Ely, but to Earith.

Vermuyden divided the Great Level into three parts, the North and Middle Levels being complete by 1651 and in 1653 the South Level was finished; this was also controversial, as in later times the three Levels sometimes worked against each other to drain what was one entity. The Old Bedford River soon failed to carry all the flood water it received. Improvements were made in 1651 by digging the New Bedford River parallel to it, so creating a large area of washes between them, acting as a reservoir to hold flood water until it could be released. Similar washes were later created for the Nene at Whittlesey and on other rivers (fig. 8.1).

At first there was satisfactory agricultural production from the newly won land, and reclaimed salt marshes near Holbeach were very fertile. However there was flooding in 1673 and tidal problems with the South Level outfall at Denver Sluice. Vermuyden had not foreseen the problem of peat shrinkage. Wet peat contains about 90 percent water, and as soon as drained it shrinks and the ground surface falls; the better the drainage the faster the wastage. In 1662 it was recorded that in dry years the dike bottoms 'rose two foot'; really, of course, the surface was sinking.

It became necessary to pump water from low-level local drains into main drains and rivers that were embanked to take water across the fen by gravity. Windmill-driven pumps were already used in the siltland, as shown on Dudgale's map of Holland dated 1672. By 1700 disaster threatened and pumps were widely introduced (fig. 8.2). Haddenham fen lay below the river and in 1727 was the first local district to employ windmills. There was a chaos of responsibility between the three levels (which lasted until 1920) and in 1713 Denver sluice broke, water backing into the South Level in times of flood. The sluice was rebuilt during 1748-50, but there were still problems with 16,000 acres (6,500 hectares) of the Middle Level, even though it had 250 windmills. In 1770 all the Middle Level lay

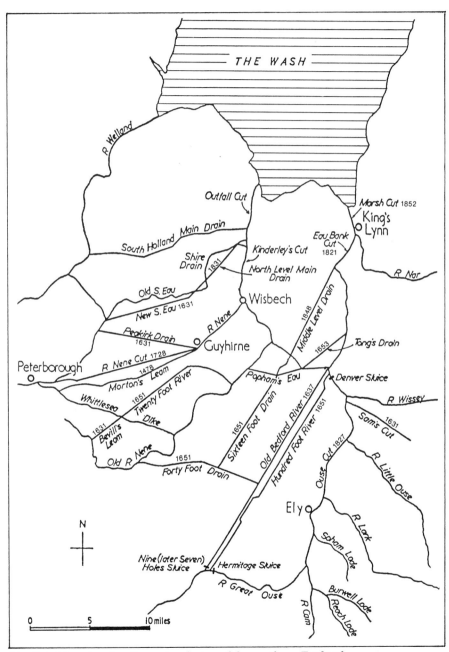

Fig. 8.1 Map showing the major drains of the southern Fenland.

*Fig. 8.2 A drainage
mill, wheel and sluice.*

under two metres of water. More attention was paid to the major river outfalls and a canal taking the Nene from Wisbech to the Wash, later called Kinderley's cut, was begun in 1720. Progress was impeded by fears about Wisbech harbour, and the canal was not completed until an Act of 1773.

As the peat continued to fall, windmills became ineffective and steam pumps were introduced. Steam was used at Sutton St Edmund in 1817 and elsewhere soon after; in Deeping Fen two steam pumps drained 25,000 acres (10,000 hectares) where 44 windmills had been. In 1812 East Fen near Stickney was drained and Midville and other parishes were created by enclosure. The Welland outfall was improved by various 19th-century acts. New main drains were cut; the North Level joining the Nene outfall at Foul Anchor (1831-4) and the Middle Level main drain was taken to the Ouse at St Germains, below Denver (1848). The improved pumping techniques, better main drains, and more effective outfalls, allowed Whittlesey Mere to be drained during 1848-52; this was the last of the great meres.

The 20th century saw administrative changes; in 1927 Conservancy Boards were placed over the local Internal Drainage Boards. The Drainage Act of 1930 set up

Catchment Boards becoming River Boards in 1948, and in 1964 River Authorities were established. The Anglian Regional Water Authority took over in 1974, being succeeded by the Environmental Agency in 1992. Steam pumps were replaced by diesel oil pumps, and these in turn were superseded by electrically driven pumps which could be turned on automatically as required, controlled by sensors monitoring water levels. Only a few of the steam pumps survive as 'industrial monuments', the 1831 pump at Stretham being notable.

The problems of exceptional weather conditions and peat shrinkage never go away (fig. 8.3). In 1913 the Ouse banks were 4 metres above mean sea level and the Spring tides usually 4.2 metres and once 5.25 metres, so if the Denver Sluice were not closed the whole South Level would flood. After heavy rain and thawing snow in 1947, combined with a North Sea storm surge, 37,000 acres (15,000 hectares) of the South Level were drowned. Since then, raised banks, improved pumps and new catchwaters have strengthened the system. The greatest quantity of floodwater to issue from the Midlands since 1947 was safely carried across the Fenland in April 1998.

Fig. 8.3 Flooding in the southern Fenland in 1862.

The reason behind all the manoeuvres toward drainage was, and is, that of increased use of the land for pasture and then agriculture. The potential richness of the first newly-drained land was soon realised, and, as we have seen, led to the complete reclamation of the Fenland in the 17th and 18th centuries. Technology was always driven forward on the promise of capital returns, often based as much on hope as certainty. Today, there is more of the former and less of the latter, but this is a reflection as much of external factors as of Fenland matters. In any event, the Fens are the poorer for it all.

In recent years, farmers have been encouraged to level land, to continue drainage, to create large fields, and to plant specialised crops. The result is the Fenland of today, with many of the archaeological monuments damaged. This was the starting point for the Fenland Survey - to recover the evidence of the past before it perished and so provide better information to reconstruct the long and complex history of the Fenland. The main events are summarised below.

8000 BC	**the Fenland basin**
	silts and peat formation
	fen edge and island occupation
	submergence of the evidence
BC/AD	**first settlement on silt**
AD 900	**first sea defences**
	fen lives recorded
AD 1600	**large-scale drainage schemes initiated**
	pasture and plots
	lifting of water and cultivation
AD 1700	**windmills and shrinkage of peat**
AD 1920	**diesel pumps**
	accelerated desiccation
AD 1950	**deeper ploughing and drainage**
AD 1980	**Fenland Project**
AD 1990	**conservation and exploitation**

There is another reason why the Fenland Survey was set up over 20 years ago. It was to identify those sites and monuments that had survived the depredations of the past centuries, especially the 20th century, and could be preserved for the interest and educational needs of the future. That the record of the past in such a vast landscape could be obliterated, leaving barely a trace, was considered to be morally and intellectually unjustifiable. So the Fenland Survey had a requirement to identify sites, to assess them from the standpoint of national significance, and to create a body of evidence and opinion that would aid local and national agencies in their efforts to protect and manage sites, and landscapes, for the future. It is too early for us to say if preservation of some of the sites we have described here will be possible, and if the measures so far adopted will be successful in the decades to come. They involve the laying-down of areas to grassland rather than for arable cultivation, the burial of sites to protect them from surface deterioration, and the retention of water levels around sites, through embankments, where drainage threatens to allow valuable evidence decay. Much has been lost in the past, much remains to be preserved for the future.

The history of the Fenland, from very early times to the present, is one of human societies grappling with and benefiting from the waters that flowed and surged into the Fenland basin. It is a story of major economic accomplishment, in settling land and exploiting natural wealth, and of many minor human disasters, in fields and houses abandoned during bad times. But now that we know the Fenland was settled and remained so over the past 6000 years, we can begin to appreciate the advantages of a Fenland existence, as well as the stubbornness of the Fenlanders – resistant to change, adhering to the way of life that had its beginnings many centuries ago. Traditions of behaviour, capitalising on the variety of resources, seasonally distinct and occasionally rich in harvest and sometimes catastrophically failing, all helped shape the character of the human societies of the Fenland. We know that much remains to be found out about these past lives, and that much has been damaged or destroyed by modern methods of drainage and cultivation. Yet many Fenlanders of today are deeply interested in the past, in retrieving the bits and pieces of ancient settlement, and in helping to preserve those monuments that have now been identified as important elements in the study of Changing Landscapes: the Ancient Fenland.

Acknowledgements

The Fenland Survey was funded by English Heritage (represented by G. J. Wainwright and P. Walker) and work was carried out by a number of organisations and individuals: Cambridgeshire (D. Hall, C. Evans and C. French), Lincolnshire (T. Lane and P. Hayes), Norfolk (R. Silvester, M. Leah and A. Crowson), Suffolk (E. Martin), and also M. Waller and F. Pryor. Cambridgeshire County Council and the Department of Archaeology, University of Cambridge, provided offices and facilities. Many other people have contributed indirectly to this book and S. C. Minnitt and D. Musgrove have assisted in its preparation. We are grateful for all the support we have received.

We also thank various organisations and individuals for permission to use their copyright illustrations:

Cambridge University Committee for Aerial Photography (figs 1.4, 5.4, 7.2).

Cambridge University Museum of Archaeology and Anthropology (figs 2.6, 3.6, 3.8, 4.3, 4.5, 6.1, 6.2).

Cambridge Archaeological Unit (fig. 4.4).

Heritage Trust of Lincolnshire (fig. 3.3).

Field Archaeology Division, Norfolk Museums Service (figs 5.6, 7.3).

Fenland Archaeological Trust (figs 2.7, 2.8).

English Heritage (figs 1.1, 1.2, 2.4, 2.5, 3.1, 4.6, 5.1, 6.3, 7.5, 7.7).

The British Museum (figs 5.2, 5.3).

Grahame Clark estate (figs 2.2, 2.9).

Chris Cox (fig. 4.7).

Charles French (fig. 3.2).

Anthony Harding (fig. 3.9).

Rog Palmer (fig. 4.8, 5.7).

Wisbech Library, Lilian Ream Exhibition Collection (fig. 6.4).

John Wymer (fig. 2.1).

Further reading

David Hall and John Coles 1994. *Fenland Survey: an essay in landscape and persistence* (English Heritage, London).

H. C. Darby 1983. *The Changing Fenland* (Cambridge).

W. Dugdale (ed. Cole) 1772. *The History of Imbanking and Draining of Divers Fens and Marshes* (London).

C. Fox 1923. *The Archaeology of the Cambridge Region* (Cambridge).

H. Godwin 1978. *Fenland: its ancient past and uncertain future* (Cambridge).

S. H. Miller and S. B. J. Skertchly 1878. *The Fenland Past and Present* (London).

F. Pryor 1991. *Flag Fen, Prehistoric Fenland Centre* (English Heritage, London).

P. Salway, S. J. Hallam and J. Bromwich 1970 (editor C. W. Phillips). *The Fenland in Roman Times* (Royal Geographical Society, London).

More details of individual sites and areas can be seen in the Fenland Survey reports, and in books on several related projects. Almost all are published in East Anglian Archaeology (EAA).

D. Hall 1987. *Fenland Project 2: Cambridgeshire Survey, Peterborough to March. EAA 35.*

D. Hall 1992. *Fenland Project 6: The South-Western Cambridgeshire Fenlands. EAA 56.*

D. Hall 1996. *Fenland Project 10: Cambridgeshire Survey, the Isle of Ely and Wisbech. EAA 79.*

P. Hayes and T. Lane 1992. *Fenland Project 5: Lincolnshire Survey, the South-west Fens. EAA 55.*

T. Lane 1993. *Fenland Project 8: Lincolnshire Survey, the Northern Fen-edge. EAA 66.*

R. Silvester 1988. *Fenland Project 3: Norfolk Survey, Marshland and the Nar Valley. EAA 45.*

R. Silvester 1991. *Fenland Project 4: Norfolk Survey, the Wissey Embayment and the Fen Causeway. EAA 52.*

F. Healy 1996. *Fenland Project 11: The Wissey Embayment: Evidence for pre-Iron Age Occupation. EAA 78.*

M. Waller 1994. *Fenland Project 9: Flandrian Environmental Change in Fenland. EAA 70.*

C. French and F. Pryor 1993. *The South-west Fen Dyke Survey project 1982-86. EAA 59.*

F. Pryor (ed.) 1985. *Fenland Project 1: The Lower Welland Valley. EAA 27.*

A. Crowson, T. Lane and J. Reeve 1998. *Fenland Management Project Excavations 1991-1995.* Lincolnshire Archaeology and Heritage Report.

Museums to visit

It will be worth telephoning in advance to get opening times and other information.

Boston: Guildhall Museum, South Street, Boston, Lincs. PE21 6HT. 01205 365954.

Bury St Edmunds: Moyse's Hall Museum, Cornhill, Bury St Edmunds, Suffolk. IP33 1DX. 01284 757488.

Cambridge: University Museum of Archaeology and Anthropology, Downing Street, Cambridge. CB2 3DZ. 01223 337733.

Ely Museum, Market Street, Ely Cambs. CB7 4LS. 01353 666655.

Ely: Stretham Old Engine, Green End Lane, Stretham, Ely, Cambs. CB6 3LF. 01353 649210 (1831 pumping house and beam engine).

March and District Museum, High Street, March, Cambs. PE15 9JJ. 01354 654783.

King's Lynn: The Lynn Museum, Old Market Street, King's Lynn. PE30 1NL. 01553 775501.

Mildenhall and District Museum, King Street, Bury St Edmunds. IP28 7EX. 01638 716970.

Norwich Castle Museum. NRL 4JU. 01603 223624.

Peterborough City Museum and Art Gallery, Priestgate. PE1 ILF. 01733 343329.

Peterborough: Flag Fen Bronze Age Excavations, Fourth Drove, Peterborough. PE1 5UR. 01733 313414.

Spalding: Ayscoughfee Hall Museum, Churchgate, Spalding. PE11 2RA.

(also responsible for Pinchbeck Marsh Engine and Land Drainage Museum (1833 steam beam engine)).

St Ives: Norris Museum, The Broadway, St Ives, Huntingdon, Cambs. PE17 4BX. 01480 465101.

Tattershall: Guardhouse Museum, Tattershall Castle, Lincoln. LN4 4LR. 01526 342 543.

Thorney Heritage Centre, The Tankyard, Station Road, Thorney, Peterborough. PE6 0QE. 01733 270780.

Wisbech and Fenland Museum, Wisbech, Cambs. PE13 1ES. 01945 583817.

Index to place names

The index below gives the National Grid Reference to the nearest kilometre square for each place. Administrative counties are distinguished by a capital letter: Cambridgeshire (C), Lincolnshire (L), Norfolk (N), Peterborough (P) and Suffolk (S).